# Praise for *Facing Decline, Finding Hope*

"Jones has courageously identified the challenge before the overwhelming majority of churches in North America. As painful as his analysis is, it remains rooted in the hope that comes from God alone. Brave Christians will read and pray!" —**Dwight Stinnett**, executive minister, American Baptist Churches of the Great Rivers Region

"Fifty years ago it didn't occur to anyone that most people would have better things to do than 'go' to church. Church (as we knew it) had intrinsic value, but no longer. The first step is admitting we have a problem. If there are twelve steps, Jones has been through them all, and sober for a long time. In *Facing Decline, Finding Hope*, Jones gives us a big book for churches in recovery which is bound to be required reading for all seminarians." —**Sean Witty**, senior minister, First Baptist Church, Newton Centre, Massachusetts

"This is a deep and insightful book on the realities faced by every church trying to stay relevant, healthy, and vital in today's ever-changing world. The response may be too simple for most of us—let go and let God lead on to a new future! How do we really do that? Jones suggests new questions that help in radically rethinking what it means to be church in a different world." —**Mayra Castañeda**, senior minister, First Baptist Church of Westfield

"Even with the decline that is facing mainline Protestantism, thousands of clergy still serve thousands of churches, and they're trying to make a difference. Based on his many years as a pastor, professor, and denominational executive, Jones brings a clear-eyed vision of how congregations can thrive and flourish, even in tough times. This book will indeed do what it promises: bring hope." —**Tony Jones**, author of *The Church is Flat*

D0681609

# FACING DECLINE, FINDING HOPE

# FACING DECLINE, FINDING HOPE

## *New Possibilities for Faithful Churches*

## Jeffrey D. Jones

## Foreword by Phyllis Tickle

An Alban Institute Book

ROWMAN & LITTLEFIELD
Lanham • Boulder • New York • London

Published by Rowman & Littlefield
A wholly owned subsidary of The Rowman & Littlefield Publishing Group, Inc.
4501 Forbes Boulevard, Suite 200, Lanham, Maryland 20706
www.rowman.com

Unit A, Whitacre Mews, 26-34 Stannary Street, London SE11 4AB

British Library Cataloguing in Publication Information Available

**Library of Congress Cataloging-in-Publication Data**

Jones, Jeffrey D.
Facing decline, finding hope : new possibilities for faithful churches / Jeffrey D. Jones.
pages cm
"An Alban Institute book."
Includes bibliographical references.
ISBN 978-1-56699-772-0 (cloth : alk. paper)—ISBN 978-1-56699-732-4 (pbk. : alk. paper)—ISBN 978-1-56699-733-1 (electronic)
1. Church attendance. 2. Church growth. 3. Church renewal. 4. Pastoral theology. 5. Church work. I. Title.
BV652.5.J66 2015
254.5—dc23

2014042142

Printed in the United States of America

To David Fredrickson, Sam Tucker, Sarah Drummond, and Peter Gomes, cherished friends and colleagues of the past decade, whose lively spirits and deep faith have enlivened my spirit and deepened my faith.

# CONTENTS

# FOREWORD

Hope is almost always seen as a good and desirable thing. It is that, of course, but sometimes the hope we seek for . . . the hope we desperately want and thirst for, in fact . . . is hidden from us by our own anguish. We are so deeply distressed in body or spirit that, like the Children of Israel overcome by serpents in the desert, we cannot look up from our agony, even when we know that by doing so we would relieve it.

Sometimes, of course, hope is obscured by the sheer franticness of our search for it. Paradoxically, our own despairing analysis of what is so desperately wrong effectively distracts us from the balm that we seek.

And sometimes it is simply fear itself that keeps us from embracing the hope we yearn for, because sometimes, to embrace the thing that will heal us means first the recasting . . . or perhaps even the casting off . . . of what we are and of how we have been. Yet, as our own Scriptures teach us, without hope, the people perish.

It is in full awareness of all these things and of the imperative patent in them that Jeffrey Jones has written the words that follow here, and it is in full awareness of all these things and of the imperative patent in them that we must read his words. A seasoned pastor and, for several years now, a seminary professor, he both knows the rhythms and contours of our contemporary lives as Christians and as Church, while also having the kind of informed impunity that allows him to challenge us into looking honestly at those contours. His is a remarkable circumstance, and this is a remarkable book.

There is no question about the fact that institutional Christianity as we have known and practiced it over the five hundred years since the Reformation is no longer consonant with the mores and norms, assumptions, means, and perceptions of the times and circumstances in which we now live. The world in which we are citizen-dwellers drives us to seek a structure and practice of faith that is less hierarchal and more communal than is that which the Reformation and the centuries since bequeathed us. It presents us with questions whose intellectual and factual undergirding was unknown—and therefore unavailable—to our religious forebears. It finds institutions themselves suspect . . . and most particularly religious ones . . . and does not hesitate to challenge them, even to their demise. It is suspicious of the professional expert and seeks instead the democratization of roles in both sacred and secular life. It assumes an easy and unfettered access both to information and to our fellow human beings. It seeks spiritual reality and presupposes open intercourse with it. And as Jones shows us in his radical, but instructive commentary on the work of Ezra and Nehemiah, it yearns, as have other times of holy upheaval, for prophets more than it does for priests. There is a bravery required just to acknowledge these changes. And certainly, even more than that, enormous bravery is required to address them. But bravery alone is not enough; for bravery, uninformed, can all too easily become foolhardy or pointlessly destructive. As you read the pages that follow, then, you indeed will find bravery in Jones's addressing of the issues of Church today, but you will find something else as well—something much more valuable and many, many times more useful. You will find an honesty of presentation about what is and an integrity of forecasting about what can (and must) be. Beyond those things, you will find as well suggestions for arriving at that state of religious health and spiritual well-being that is our hope. You will, in other words, find a most hope-filled wisdom.

Phyllis Tickle

# PREFACE

This book grew out of my experience as a pastor, interim pastor, and denominational executive. It is very much a product of my own peculiar view of the world and the church in these days. There are those who have been important in helping to shape that view, however. I very much appreciate the insights they have provided to broaden my own vision and provide a more solid grounding for that vision.

Initial discussions with faculty colleagues Beth Nordbeck and Greg Mobley provided both affirmation and direction. Ongoing conversations with Jennifer Peace and Adam Hearlson offered encouragement, insight, and time to laugh, all of which were essential to my thinking and writing.

I am grateful to Dean Sarah Drummond for graciously providing time away from my other responsibilities to write and supporting my work in untold other ways.

Phyllis Tickle, in her wondrously energetic and affirming way, provided encouragement at several key points in the writing process, assuring me that I was indeed working on something that was worth writing. She and Walter Brueggemann were especially helpful for my foray into post-Exilic history and biblical interpretation.

Dave Fredrickson, the Episcopal rector in my town, has been a consistent conversation partner and soul friend during the past several years. He has listened to my developing thoughts, abided my sometimes rather cynical humor, and offered regular and important insights for my own life and faith, as well as the content of this book. I once heard Phyllis Tickle say that whatever might emerge as church in the future would likely be some kind of "bapto-episcopal" thing. If that's true, then whatever Dave and I have been up to might be more groundbreaking than either of us imagine.

This book probably would not have been written at all if I hadn't run into Beth Gaede, the editor of my previous book. At dinner one night she asked what issues I was pondering and immediately began to encourage me to write about them. Along the way she helped design a format in which my then rather disorganized thoughts could be presented, and has been, as in the past, a perceptive editor of the manuscript I produced.

Writing can be difficult. Rewriting is often, at least for me, torturous. It takes a special person with a special kind of love to continue to accept and support someone constantly bemoaning the torturous difficulties of his life. That special person for me is my wife, Judy. Happily the days of writing and rewriting are over, but I remain grateful for her continued love and support through all the experiences of our life together.

Each of these people contributed to the process of writing this book in important ways. It is quite likely, however, that none of them would write what I have written or in the way I have written it. They might even shudder at some of it. For this final product I take full responsibility.

# INTRODUCTION

I don't need to tell you we live in difficult and precarious times. If you are looking at this book you know that most congregations are uncertain about their future. Some worry about surviving. Others wonder what they will need to be like to minister in the future. Nearly all are attempting to discover what it means to be church in this time of radical and rapid change and if they really can be that.

We live in a liminal time—a time betwixt and between. Virtually all the old answers about what it means to be and do church don't work anymore. These were not bad answers or the wrong way of doing things. Congregational leaders who used them to shape their ministry were not stupid or faithless. Rather, the world in which those answers were valid doesn't exist anymore. The challenge we face is that there are as yet no new answers—notions perhaps, but not answers. This book is about coping with this frustrating and difficult situation, which is one of the primary reasons most traditional churches are getting smaller.

I didn't think I would write another book, but this one sneaked up on me. Over the past few years I've become more aware of the radical nature of the time in which we live. We have heard a great deal about the decline of Christendom, the rise of postmodernity, and the impact of new technologies. All of these contribute to the emergence of a world that doesn't look at all like the one that existed just a few years ago. This new and ever-changing world demands change on our part, but the exact nature of the change that is needed isn't clear. I have also heard more and more church leaders talk with sadness and often frustration about the struggles they are facing as they attempt to adjust to this new world. They have read a good number of books about turnaround churches and congregational transformation. They have heard all the stories about turnaround churches that their denominational leaders tell. They have attended the workshops offered by turnaround pastors who told stories of the great success they had. But none of these proved helpful. What worked in other churches didn't seem to make any difference in their church. No matter how excited they were about the potential they began to see, it seemed impossible to excite or even interest others. Often, instead of helping, all the reading they did and workshops they attended added to their frustration, reinforcing a nagging fear that perhaps they didn't know enough, try enough, care enough; that they were failures. None of it was speaking to what perhaps had started out as a vague and amorphous notion about their church and was gradually turning into a gnawing concern. Somehow, deep down inside they had a sense that no matter what they did the chances of the congregation they served surviving another ten or perhaps twenty years was not great. And they began to sense this notion wasn't just a fatalistic pessimism brought on by their frustration, but an appropriate and reasonable insight.

Other leaders, in what would by just about any standard be considered thriving congregations, were beginning to sense that what they were doing was not sustainable—at least not over a long period of time. It might bring increased attendance and balanced budgets for a while, perhaps even a decade or two, but unless something more radical happened in the life and ministry of the congregation this would not continue. Again, this nagging concern wasn't fatalism, but a deep wondering about their leadership and their church based in an awareness that something was amiss in what they were about, that the ways they had been doing church, even though they were producing good results at present, would not be able to maintain the congregation in the manner to which it had become accustomed. Those were the realities that sneaked up on me and led to a decision to write a different kind of book about how congregations can faithfully and effectively face and respond to all the newness that today's world presents to them.

None of us knows what the future will be like. The world is changing so radically and rapidly that any attempt to tailor our ministry to assumptions we make about the future is foolhardy. What we can know at least partly is what the present is like. If our ministry responds to the realities of the present, it will be a significant improvement over continuing to respond to the realities of the past, which is what many congregations are doing. It may be that some of what we do will be part of the future. It is just as likely, however, that we will discover that some of it does not make sense for the future of the church and will be among those things we leave behind. In either case, we will be participating in the challenging work of moving ourselves and the church into an as yet unknown future, a future that God has in store for us, the church, and all creation.

This book is about dealing with the challenge of shaping the future, especially in the significant number of congregations with declining membership and which therefore might not feel all that positive about the future. Even in congregations that still have a significant number of people in worship every Sunday, the decline in membership impacts their sense of the present and hope for the future. The decline congregations are experiencing is, more often than not, a symptom of the radically different world in which we now find ourselves. While declining membership seems to make the challenge we face even greater because it reduces the resources that are available, it in fact offers an opportunity for seeing the world as it is and responding in new ways. Viewed in this way, the purpose of this book is to help leaders (both clergy and laity) in congregations that are getting smaller (regardless of their current size) face the difficult reality of decline and possible eventual death, on the one hand, and the hopeful reality that God is calling them to a new future, on the other. Clergy are the primary audience, because they are essential participants in the process of moving congregations to this new perspective on their life and ministry. There can be no doubt that if they are not on board no significant change will happen. More than that, however, clergy are often the ones who have thought deeply and long enough about congregations to understand the depth of the challenge we are facing today. This means, among other things, that they understand that more books about redevelopment, renewal, and transformation that seem to provide a formula for success are not needed. What they are looking for, and what this book seeks to provide, is an honest acknowledgment of the dim prospects for the survival of many congregations coupled with a realistic understanding of the possibilities that lie before us.

We'll do that by first looking at two significant obstacles that congregations confront today (the difficulty of facing troubling realities and a focus on institutions) in part 1. In part 2, we will explore five questions that can provide a focus for our ministry and have the potential to align us more fully with both the realities of the world and the mission of God. Finally, in part 3 we will explore the struggles that we will likely encounter along the way and consider what it will take to make our way through them.

The core concern in all of this is doing what we can do to remain faithful in ministry, no matter the situation in which we find ourselves or the amount of time we have. Recognizing the obstacles, asking the new questions, and preparing ourselves to face the struggles all contribute to our ability to remain faithful. That, even more than results, is what truly matters.

There are those who think I am pessimistic about the church, that I dwell too much on the difficulties congregations face and don't look at all the good things that are happening. There may be some truth in that. I do, however, recognize and cherish the many wondrous experiences, miracles even, that happen in countless local congregations day after day, even if those congregations are struggling to survive, facing budget challenges, and engaged in conflict. That being said, in all honesty I also think many of the so-called good things that get talked about are simply Band-Aids that will eventually lose whatever effectiveness they appear to have. More than one congregation that was once termed "a turnaround church" is now facing challenging questions of survival. I am not pessimistic, however. I believe that God is up to something great. It's just that in order to share in this great thing, we, like people of faith throughout the millennia, need to struggle with the hard realities of this world. We need perhaps to suffer because of those realities, so that we will be better able to rid ourselves of all that keeps us from God's work in this time when the former ways of doing no longer suffice. That work is, after all, the reason the church exists.

There are also some who think I tend to be cynical about the church. I think rather that I have a healthy sense of irony. You will see evidence of it if you continue to read this book. I have found, for me at least, that this sense of the ironic and the humor that flows from it help me avoid a naïve and unwarranted optimism, on the one hand, and a debilitating pessimism, on the other. This healthy irony shows itself most often in what I hope is seen as wry humor. Margaret Wheatley, in her book *So Far From Home*, talks about the importance of maintaining this type of humor for leading in situations that are so difficult they seem impossible.[1] I agree with her. It is one of the ways I keep going.

So, this is not a pessimistic book, even though it faces the reality that many congregations will not survive the next few decades. It is a hopeful book because it provides reasons to be faithful even if the survival of your congregation is doubtful. Of course, I recognize that closing a church can be a difficult and painful process, but even then there is reason for hope as God continues to be at work. It is a hopeful book because it does not assume that the only option for declining congregations is institutional hospice care. Of course, I also recognize that may be what is needed in some situations, but death never has the final word. It is a hopeful book because it is written in the deep conviction that God is up to something and that something is great. It is a hopeful book because it assumes that this thing God is up to is, as it always has been, about bringing God's reign into greater reality on earth. This is a hopeful book because it is written in the conviction that even a declining congregation that is not optimistic about its future can still be a crucible of hope.

# Part 1

# Confronting Difficult News

# PART I INTRODUCTION

**W**e need to get our heads around two major issues before we can proceed. The first issue is that congregations, denominations, and most religious institutions steadfastly avoid the bad news that we always need to face before good news can be proclaimed. In chapter 1, we will look at the reasons for that and suggest some ways to overcome this rather natural, but still not very helpful, human tendency.

The second issue is a bit more complex and will take us first into the history of Israel at the time of the return from Exile, and then to the insights of several contemporary writers about institutions and the church into today's world. While the excursion into historical Israel may at first seem to have little relationship to contemporary concerns, it will, I believe, help us see today in a new perspective. I want to warn you ahead of time that as we do this we will be challenging a well-established interpretation of the important role Ezra and Nehemiah played in the restoration of the temple and the nation. While I certainly see merit in the usual interpretation, I also see another possible perspective. As we engage this perspective, it will raise significant questions for us about the role of institutions in the mission of God and the importance, or lack thereof, of institutional survival. In a time when the survival of many congregations and other religious institutions is threatened, these are important questions for us to consider. Doing so may well help us develop a broader understanding of how to determine and assess what we are about in ministry. I will make the suggestion that one possible way to look at both Ezra and Nehemiah is that they, like many in the church today, didn't fully understand the times in which they lived and because of that misunderstanding acted in ways that thwarted rather than enhanced the mission of God in the world. At the very least, there was another option available to them that might have been considered. We will explore this in chapter 2, and then in chapter 3 look at some contemporary writers who provide a similar perspective. In many ways chapters 2 and 3 will be an exercise in facing some of the difficult possibilities we prefer to avoid that we considered in chapter 1.

If you already believe these two insights are valid, you can skip this section and move right on to the next. If, however, you are not too sure about them, spending a bit of time here will help you grasp the importance and wisdom of the succeeding sections.

# I

# THE PROBLEM WITH POOL TABLES AND WHAT THAT MEANS FOR US

The musical *The Music Man* tells the story of Professor Harold Hill, who earned his living as a traveling salesman, selling musical instruments and the promise that purchasers could learn to play them using the "think method." In order to work this con, he had to instill fear in the people of each town he worked in by convincing them that they were facing a crisis that could be resolved by the development of a boys' band. In River City, Iowa, he decided the crisis would be the new pool table that had just arrived in town. And so, in the song "Trouble," he warned the town folk of the catastrophic consequences they faced because they were refusing to acknowledge the impending disaster brought upon by that pool table.

Sometimes even con men speak the truth. In fact, their ability to make believers of people often taps into something people believe to be true in general, even if it doesn't necessarily apply to their particular situation. Whether or not the presence of a pool table in River City indicated a potential disaster is open to question. What isn't is the fact that people do close their eyes to situations they do not wish to acknowledge and choose to remain blissfully unaware of difficulties that surround them. I remember, for example, my own refusal to acknowledge a difficult situation the time I returned to my apartment to find the door open and the stereo system gone. Something inside me impelled me to go back out into the hall, close the door, and enter the apartment again, somehow believing that the situation would change if I did!

Churches are not immune to this behavior. The sad truth is that what goes on in many, if not most, churches is quite often little more than an exercise in corporate delusion. All too often, everyone conspires, perhaps unknowingly but certainly without acknowledging it, to avoid those issues that if faced would require profound and radical change in the church—from its structure to its ministry to its worship, even to its need for a building. And yet, it is only in facing these issues that congregations can find genuine reason for hope. If a congregation is to become a crucible of hope, it will need to undertake a journey through the valley of the shadow of death where we face all fears and threats. There is something essentially Christian about this process. One might even see it as a process of death and resurrection. And yet many congregations are reluctant to do this. It is almost as if they don't believe their own stuff.

Some of these hard truths churches avoid are theological, such as:

- The purpose of the church is *not* to ensure safe passage to heaven.
- Death always precedes resurrection.

Some of them are about biblical teaching, such as:

- Money is a theological issue, because it is the primary indicator of what one worships; that is, what one relies on to bring meaning, purpose, and security.
- Growing disparity between rich and poor is sin that the Bible repeatedly makes clear is reason for God's judgment.
- You look in vain through the Bible to find any indication that the purpose of the church is to maintain a building, historic or otherwise.

Some of them are about the life of the congregation, such as:

- The world has so radically changed in the past fifty years that without comparable radical change congregations are destined to slow death.

- The church can never again be what it used to be.
- Bake sales and ham dinners are not the solution to a budget short-fall.
- A budget crisis is never a financial issue; it is always an issue of identity and mission.
- Old power groups rarely change their view about the way a congregation should be; new ways of being will only arise when they no longer have power.
- The more inwardly focused a struggling church becomes, the less likely it will survive.

And some of them are very specifically about a congregation, such as:

- We pay our pastor an unconscionably low salary and justify it by saying he or she has done nothing to grow the church and increase giving, and with the belief that many of us live on fixed incomes.
- The lack of maintenance on our building makes it not only unattractive, but also an ever-increasing safety hazard.
- The chances of our church surviving another ten years are exceedingly slim, but we do not want to face the changes that might make it possible.
- The surest way to halt a discussion of anything is to say, "If you do that I'll leave the church."

Confronting these issues is difficult for everyone, even for churches that seem to have little reason to fret. You would think that more stable and financially secure churches might have the freedom to explore significant issues that could lead to change. Some do this and do it well, but more often than not these churches simply choose to remain ignorant, trusting that the harsh realities struggling churches have to deal with need not concern them. In many cases, the more worldly resources a church has, the less likely it is to face the struggles that indicate the places God is at work in the world today. If it has a large endowment, wealthy members, a still-viable reputation, it is more insulated from reality than a church that is struggling to survive. One of the important insights of liberation theology is that those in positions of privilege often lack the ability to see the harsh realities of the world that can only be engaged by those who suffer and struggle. It is not impossible for the privileged, but it is difficult—maybe like a camel going through the eye of a needle.

Congregations with abundant resources are much more likely to focus on

- institutional well-being;
- building upkeep;
- worldly standards of success;
- developing programs for parishioners;
- maintaining old traditions and styles;
- their own ability to do whatever needs to be done.

They are much less likely to

- engage with the least and the lost, the marginalized and the outsider (except to send them money or do a periodic good deed for them);
- rely on God and grace rather than themselves and their own goodness;
- radically rethink what it means to be a church in this radically different world.

And yet, if these churches can honestly confront and respond to the realities of the changing world in which we live, fundamentally readjust their understanding of the church and its ministry and mission, their future is bright, for they will have the spiritual, missional, and financial resources to thrive. Congregations that make this adjustment are destined to be an important part of the future, even if they are not as large as they once were.

Although some congregations with significant resources may simply delay facing the harsh financial realities that lead other congregations to struggle, a congregation's being without substantial resources certainly doesn't guarantee that it will meet this challenge any better. The truth is many, if not most, struggling churches don't deal with these concerns either. Churches struggling to survive have an array of rationales for playing it safe and avoiding the issues and dynamics that call their ability to survive into question. There is often an addiction-like dynamic at work. Denial continues until the church hits bottom. And then it is usually too late to do anything. All but seemingly impossible alternatives have disappeared. In the meantime, the members of the congregation often use excuses, blaming, or just plain avoidance to ignore the issues that are essential to their well-being. More than twenty years ago, Tom Bandy published a book entitled *Kicking Habits: Welcome Relief for Addicted Churches.*[1] There were many who had a strong negative reaction to the notion that addictive behavior is present in churches and keeping them from being what they are called to be. I think, however, he was right and the events of the past twenty years provide some pretty strong evidence of that.

Knowing a bit about what lies behind this need to avoid and deny can help us move beyond it, so let's look at some of those dynamics.

Our well-being depends upon our ability to make meaning out of our experience. Among the resources many draw on for doing this are the religious symbols and practices we use to order our lives and interpret what happens to us. The regularity of Sunday worship, the conviction that God is with us and will protect us, the pattern of hymns and prayers that have been part of life since childhood, traditional beliefs about heaven and what it means to live a faithful life, even the church building in which marriages and funerals of loved ones have taken place all contribute to a system that offers continuity and stability because they provide a frame-work of meaning making. Anthropologist Clifford Geertz explains it this way: "Sacred symbols function to synthesize a people's ethos—the tone, character, and quality of their life, its moral and aesthetic style and mood—and their world view—the picture they have of the way things in sheer actuality are, their most comprehensive ideas of order."[2] This works well until the symbols begin to lose their power.

> The thing we seem least able to tolerate is a threat to our powers of conception, a suggestion that our ability to create, grasp and use sym-bols may fail us. . . . [We depend] upon symbols and symbol systems

with a dependence so great as to be decisive for [our] creatural viability and, as a result, [our] sensitivity to even the remotest indication that they may prove unable to cope with one or another aspect of experience raises with [us] the gravest sort of anxiety.[3]

This is the reality we are facing in this liminal time. When traditional symbols no longer play this role we become anxious, which in turn leads to denial and a variety of other less-than-healthy behaviors. Anxiety is a bear. No one enjoys it. Organizations can't abide it. One of the key insights of systems theory is that all systems work to seek homeostasis, so any threat of change creates anxiety. When we live in a world of constant, rapid, and radical change, that anxiety becomes chronic. When it does, it overwhelms us to a point that we need to find ways to deal with it that will restore some measure of coherence and equilibrium to our lives. One way to deal with anxiety is to attempt to ignore its causes. This, of course, takes a great amount of effort, psychic and otherwise, and it is ultimately a losing battle, but we do it nonetheless. There are, I am quite certain, countless congregations for which the financial trends provide solid evidence that they do not have the money needed to survive but that are simply content to do whatever they can to pay the bills each month without giving a thought to what will happen in six months or a year. Peter Steinke, in writing about this aspect of a system's response to anxiety, notes:

> Strange as it seems, some anxious congregations refuse to *see* their problems. People have a strong tendency to deny troubles—as if the difficulties should not be present, as if "Don't disturb" signs are hung on every door. Not recognizing a problem is an anxious defense. As pressure mounts, people's blindness may give way to begrudging acknowledgement. Even then, the congregation's reticence to act may be equal to their resistance to see. Still, anxiety denied has a habit of staying around and festering.[4]

When denial no longer works and the festering begins, other symptoms begin to appear. Steinke points to several of them, but the possibilities seem endless. They include: oversimplifying, seeking quick fixes, freezing, scapegoating, and holding the congregation hostage to threats. All of these are reactive responses to anxiety that develop when denial is no longer possible. All of them consume a congregation and make faithful ministry and mission impossible.

In their books *How the Way We Talk Can Change the Way We Work* and *Immunity to Change*, Robert Kegan and Lisa Laskow Lahey provide a perspective on change that brings an added dimension to the issue of denial and the other ways in which anxiety is handled.[5] They remind us of the importance of competing commitments in shaping our behavior. This occurs when two commitments we hold are incompatible. They compete with each other in our thinking and often make decision making impossible because we do not want to reject either one. Members of a congregation, for example, may have a genuine commitment to engagement with the world in God's mission. They may sincerely want to make changes in the way they do things that will make that engagement possible, and yet they continue to act in ways that make these changes impossible. They are not being hypocrites or deceptive, but rather other genuine commitments, often unstated and unconscious, are blocking the needed behavior. They may also have a competing commitment to being a peaceful community that does not engage in conflict or a commitment to honor the legacy of a former beloved pastor and her style of ministry. So, fearing the decision about mission will lead to conflict or a denial of the congregation's heritage, they continually act in ways that make change impossible. None of the commitments is necessarily wrong, but they are competing. In order to resolve the conflict between the commitments, the unspoken, unconscious commitments need to be acknowledged so that the congregation can consider how to honor them in a different way or set them aside so that change is possible. Often, however, the thought of having this discussion creates enough anxiety among people in congregations that they avoid it all together. We all have competing commitments that block action in areas that are important to us. When we understand this, we are less likely to judge those who appear to oppose change, more likely to work with them to consider ways in which movement can take place without undermining either commitment, or determine that the unspoken commitment is one that now needs to be set aside. To do this, however, all of us will need to acknowledge the competing commitments that we hold.

The chilling story of Ananias and Sapphira in Acts 5 provides a significant insight for us as we consider the importance of honestly and earnestly facing reality. It's a story about money, but it speaks to our concerns as well. Ananias and Sapphira had held back some of the money they received from the sale of their property, instead of giving it to the community, as was the practice in the early church. Peter abruptly confronted first Ananias and then Sapphira with their deceptive behavior and the lie they told to cover it up. Clearly, facing this was not an easy thing to do, for either Peter or them. In fact, it was so hard for them that they each in turn dropped dead. Certainly this reaction is not something any of us would seek in our congregations! However, the story does make a point about the importance of facing reality in the church. This becomes even clearer when we realize, as William Willimon notes, that immediately following this account, Luke uses the word *church* for the very first time.[6] Can it be that truth telling, facing difficult realities, is in fact essential to being a church?

Given both the difficulty and importance all of us individually and together have in facing harsh realities, we need to devote some time to considering what we as leaders in the church can do to enhance the possibilities of being able to do this. Here are a few approaches that can be helpful.

*Be a nonanxious presence.* A congregation in denial is always a place of anxiety, usually both chronic and acute. An anxious system is in need of a calming presence, someone who is not reactive. That person, in systems theory, provides a "nonanxious presence." The key here is not that the leader can never be anxious, fearful, angry, or hurt, but that the leader does not act out of those feelings. Steinke again provides an insight: "The non-anxious presence is a description of how a person works to keep the center of control within oneself and as a way to affect relationships in a positive manner. To be a non-anxious presence, you focus on your own behavior and its modification rather than being preoccupied with how others function."[7] Being nonanxious, quite obviously, is easier said than done, but it does provide an image for us of the way we might conduct ourselves as leaders in order to move a congregation beyond denial and delusion because it provides a steadying, focused presence. We'll look at this a bit more in chapter 9.

*Create a holding place.* Among the many helpful leadership strategies that Ronald Heifetz and Marty Linsky offer in *Leadership on the Line* is the creation of a holding environment. It may prove to be particularly helpful in moving a congregation beyond denial. According to Heifetz and Linsky:

> A holding environment is a place where there is enough cohesion to offset the centrifugal forces that arise when people [are faced with significant challenges]. In a holding environment, with structural, procedural, or virtual boundaries, people feel safe enough to address problems that are difficult, not only because they strain ingenuity, but also because they strain relationships.[8]

Acknowledging that holding environments will look and feel quite different in different contexts, they offer the following possibilities:

- a protected physical space you create by hiring an outside consultant;
- a group's working off-site;
- the shared language and common history of a community;
- deep trust in an institution;
- a clear set of rules and processes that give minority voices the confidence that they will be heard.[9]

*Affirm enduring values and beliefs.* In the face of so much that challenges the way things are and what people hold dear, that creates disarray and dislocation, that overwhelms and perhaps even crushes the spirit, it is vital to affirm those things that will last. In many congregations, worship can be the time and place for that. Too often worship has been the reason for conflict in congregations, as it has been the focus of the need to change. Might it more effectively and faithfully be used as a time and place for affirming what will endure, despite all the change that is taking place? Liturgical traditions perhaps have the advantage here, but nonliturgical traditions can still utilize the worship experience in this way. This can be a time to lift up the continuing love, compassion, and grace of God; God's powerful presence in our lives; the ways in which God seeks us and always welcomes us home. If worship is a time of praise and thanksgiving, of affirmation, of enduring biblical insights, it can be the secure point in what might otherwise be a chaotic world. And if it is that, those who participate can be more open to facing the chaos they encounter elsewhere.

For many congregations, fear and anxiety lead to a compelling desire to deny. But, this corporate delusion inevitably leads to slow death. It places a congregation at the mercy of those very forces they attempt to avoid facing. There is, however, a word for those who find themselves in situations such as these. It is a word of assurance—a word that affirms a faith that is strong enough to halt the habits of avoidance and denial and stop seeking sustenance where it cannot be found. The word comes from the prophet Isaiah:

> Ho, everyone who thirsts,
> come to the waters;
> and you that have no money,
> come, buy and eat!
> Come, buy wine and milk
> without money and without price.
> Why do you spend your money for that which is not bread,
> and your labor for that which does not satisfy?
> Listen carefully to me, and eat what is good,
> and delight yourself in rich food.
> Incline your ear, and come to me;
> listen, so that you may live.
> I will make with you an everlasting covenant,
> my steadfast, sure love for David.
>
> (Isaiah 55:1–3)

If we trust this word, we are able to move beyond the fears we do not want to face so our congregations can become not dens of delusion, but crucibles of hope.

# 2

# WHY EZRA AND NEHEMIAH WERE WRONG AND WHAT THAT MEANS FOR US

In this chapter we will take a brief trip to the fifth century BCE. In the next chapter we will follow that up with a look at a number of contemporary writers who will help us build some connections between that time and our own. I hope you will find the political intrigues of ancient Israel interesting, if not fascinating, for I believe they provide a picture of the ways in which people of faith seek to be faithful in a difficult time. This picture offers some important insights for us in our difficult time.

## A TALE OF PRIEST AND PROPHET

Despite the high esteem in which they are held, Ezra and Nehemiah were wrong.

Okay, I admit that's a bit of an overstatement. Ezra and Nehemiah were not really wrong about everything. Appointed by the Persian king, Artaxerxes, to go to Jerusalem following the Exile in Babylon, they were instrumental in reestablishing the political and religious structure of the nation. In doing this they contributed in significant ways to the continuation of the traditional worship of Israel and the development of a civic community following the disarray of the Exile. Ezra is traditionally recognized as the person responsible for the establishment of the Torah as the central document of Jewish faith. Nehemiah is credited with rebuilding the city walls. Without taking anything away from these significant accomplishments, I do want to raise some questions about the vision that guided their work and its relationship to the mission of God in the world—questions we should be asking ourselves in this time of radical and rapid change and dislocation that bears some striking similarities to the time they lived. We, like them, live in a time in which many respond to the disarray we face with determined efforts to revitalize what has been, to redevelop and renew it. There is much that can be said for this, but a careful study of the experience of the Return and Reconstruction provides another important perspective. I am intrigued that based on the traditional understanding of the role Nehemiah played in the rebuilding of Jerusalem at least two mainline denominations named their congregational revitalization efforts after him. But there is, I think, a measure of irony in this given the fact that Nehemiah was also responsible for rebuilding the walls of the city. If there is anything the church needs today it is not new walls! So, perhaps a new perspective on the work of Ezra and Nehemiah would be helpful to us and provide additional insight into the challenges we face.

In this chapter I would like to set aside the traditional view of Ezra and Nehemiah, at least for a while. There is, I believe good reason to question the wisdom of their efforts in rebuilding old institutions, especially when the result of those efforts paled in comparison to what had been before.

Here's the shorthand, radically overstated version of my theory about a different way to look at the work of Ezra and Nehemiah: one of the things God was up to in the Exile was systematically destroying the old institutions of religion because they no longer served God's mission, but instead themselves and the religion they had created. That's why Isaiah in Exile proclaimed that God was doing a new thing. But, once the exiles (or at least some of them) returned to Jerusalem they almost immediately set about rebuilding the old institutions. It is as if they missed the point of everything they had been through. Both Ezra and Nehemiah fit into that rebuilding effort, helping to ensure its successful completion. Yes, the temple did last another five hundred years (and that can be seen as a worthy accomplishment), but ultimately it was destroyed and "new things" did emerge in both the further development of the synagogue as the center of worship and in the emergence of Christianity. But it took five hundred years.

There, I've said it straight out. Now you know where my bias lies!

What might have happened if Ezra and Nehemiah and those who joined with them had understood what God was up to in their world and the potential of the time in which they lived in a different way? What might have happened if they had devoted themselves to doing a new thing instead of rebuilding old institutions?

There are, I admit, a number of problems with this interpretation. The precise history of the time and of the work of Ezra and Nehemiah is difficult to determine. Haggai, Zechariah, and Zerubbabel are perhaps clearer examples of the focus on rebuilding the temple. The interpretation I offer ignores the complexity of the Bible, its varying perspectives, and its diverse understandings of the work of God in the world. It avoids important subtleties and nuances that provide deeper insight into the events that occurred in Jerusalem following the Return. It is based on the heretical premise of my having some kind of exclusive insight into what God was up to in the Exile. (That's why I said it was radically overstated!) I admit all that, but I hope the way I have stated it has gotten your attention. Please understand, while I do raise some significant questions about their work, Ezra and Nehemiah are not the villains of this piece. I have chosen them simply because they, of all the leaders of the time, are seen as most responsible for rebuilding the temple and the old order. That's not bad, but it does raise some interesting and provocative questions for our situation today.

Now that we have a picture of the issues to explore, let's take a more reflective and disciplined approach to the events in sixth- and fifth-century BCE Jerusalem.

The Exile was a time of monumental disruption, destruction, and dislocation. With the defeat of Jerusalem, the destruction of the temple, the demise of the Davidic monarchy, and the deportation of the nation's leading citizenry to Babylon in 587 BCE, everything the people had relied on to provide meaning and security for their lives was gone. If that weren't enough, the most basic claims about God that served as the foundation of their religious life, of their concept of nationhood, and of their identity as a people no longer seemed valid. God would not or could not protect them. The nation and, it seemed, the God on whom they relied had been vanquished.

Jeremiah and other prophets had offered reasons for this profound destruction and a warning that it would happen, but the people and their leaders had preferred the messages of those who offered hopeful platitudes and pious assurances of God's protection and favor. Few had listened to the warnings of Jeremiah, for the notion that Israel's sin was the reason for their defeat and exile was a difficult one to accept. Babylon triumphed, in Jeremiah's view, because this empire was doing the work of God in bringing Israel to task. But times change and empires fall; God's work gets done in different ways. Sensing this was a new time requiring a new message, a new prophet arose, most likely in Babylon, to bring a word of hope. The one we know as Second Isaiah called on the people to be a part of the new thing God was set to do. Following Persia's conquest of Babylon, Cyrus issued an edict allowing those who had been deported to return to Jerusalem. Some did.

The return to Jerusalem, however, led, not to a unity of faith and practice among the people of Israel, but to political infighting among religious groups seeking to shape the life and faith of the nation. This power struggle was at times intense as it pitted two long-standing faith traditions against each other—one based in the hierarchical priesthood and the other in the visionary prophets. The work of Ezra and Nehemiah led to the final triumph of the priestly tradition and to the demise of the prophetic tradition. These results are the reason the events of this time— the conflict between priest and prophet, between rebuilding the old and doing the new—are particularly important for us.[1] What the two sides were about in this controversy and the way in which it was resolved, although not the same as the issues we face, offer an intriguing and potentially insightful perspective from which to view our own time.

The prophetic tradition looked primarily to Second Isaiah and his proclamation of a hope to be realized in the not-too-distance future with the coming of the reign of God. The priestly tradition focused on the temple as the central feature of Israel's religious life, claiming that proper cultic practice ensured an ongoing right relationship with Yahweh.

Each group had its own program for restoration. The priestly program emphasized the reestablishment of the old structures and offices of the nation, particularly in its religious life. Believing that economic dislocation, injustice, and other suffering resulted from the lack of a pure cultic practice, it stressed the ordering of religious life and leadership according to the traditional ways of the temple. This focus on the elite priesthood, they believed, would eventually benefit all. In his significant work on the history of this time, *The Dawn of Apocalyptic*, Hebrew Bible scholar Paul Hanson explains:

> The deplorable economic and social conditions of the land could be changed only if the root of the problem was addressed. For what the land was experiencing was more than a poor harvest or a dry season; it was experiencing divine curse! The nerve center of the nation, indeed of the cosmos, had to be restored to its proper order, and this could occur only if the temple, which was the earthly center of the cult and the mundane counterpart to the heavenly temple, were rebuilt and its sacrificial systems brought back into full operation. [2]

The priestly approach was in many respects a trickle-down religiosity.

The specifics of the priestly restoration strategy evolved over time with changing circumstances, as did the visionary strategy of the prophetic tradition. Its various expressions can be found in Haggai and Zechariah. But perhaps its most thorough description is found in Ezekiel 40 to 48. Their strategy called for:

- the rebuilding of the temple;
- the reestablishment of a priesthood with the descendants of Zadok, who had primacy in the temple prior to the Exile;
- the reestablishment of the Davidic royal line;

- the taking on of the traditional kingly and priestly roles by Zerubab-
bel (of the Davidic line) and Joshua (of the Zadokite line).

The prophetic proposal, at least in its early form, is most concisely
summarized in the work of Third Isaiah, specifically Isaiah 60 to 62.
Written in Jerusalem shortly after the return, these words offered a promise of a restored land in which the people would know the full glory that
comes from being chosen by God. Isaiah promised a restoration of the
nation (Isaiah 60:1–9) and described the way in which the promise will
become reality:

> The walls and sanctuary would be rebuilt and the city secured by the
> destruction of enemies (Isaiah 60:10–12).
> A new order of peace, righteousness, and salvation would be estab-
> lished (Isaiah 60:17–18).
> The traditional offices held by the elite would be democratized (Isaiah
> 61:6).

All of this would be accomplished in order to "bring good news to the
oppressed, to bind up the brokenhearted, to proclaim liberty to the cap-
tives, and release to the prisoners; to proclaim the year of the Lord's
favor, and the day of vengeance of our God; to comfort all who mourn"
(Isaiah 61:1–2). In the visionary program, Yahweh was the one who
would accomplish all of this.

Hanson summarizes the contrasting programs of the two groups in this
way:

1. The leaders of the prophetic community are Peace and Righteousness (Isaiah 60:17b), those of the hierocracy are the various offi-
   cials of the priestly and civil hierarchies. . . .
2. The promise of the visionary is that *the whole nation* "will be
   named priests of Yahweh. . ."; the [priestly] carefully regulates . . .
   "those who may be admitted to the temple and all those who are to
   be excluded. . . ."

3. The visionary exults, "Your people shall all be righteous" (60:21); the realist meticulously explains that holiness is reserved for the few. . . .

4. The visionary announces: "The glory of Lebanon will come to you . . . to adorn the site of my sanctuary . . . ; the realist draws up architectural plans, exact in every detail, for the new temple, and lays it before the people to build it.[3]

In the years after the return, the priestly sect gradually asserted its authority by taking advantage of a weakened Persia to play on Israel's nationalistic feelings and cleverly adopting prophetic imagery for their own purposes. Including in their proclamation the eschatological fervor that in the past had been exclusively a characteristic of the prophets brought a visionary dimension to their realistic message.

As the priestly group reestablished the structures and leadership of the preexilic nation, consolidating its rule and power to the exclusion of other groups, the prophetic/visionary group became more and more disillusioned. For the prophetic group this was not simply a matter of losing a power struggle, however. In their view the strategy of the priestly group undermined one of the basic dimensions of Israelite faith. Previously, the prophets of Israel served an independent role that was essential to the well-being of the nation. They provided a check on the kingship by challenging the decisions and actions of the king when these seemed out of line with the prophets' understanding of what it meant to be faithful to God. Haggai and Zechariah, however, as they furthered the work of the priestly group, used the tools of the prophet to support the existing political system. In that they provided a divine sanction for a human institution and denied the unique role the prophets were intended to play in the fabric of the nation. The result of this was that the traditional prophetic concern for mercy and justice gave way to a concern for power and control supporting the reestablishment of the preexilic religious and political structures.[4]

This turn of events, quite naturally, brought a reaction from the prophetic group. At first they escalated their critique of the priestly program and its cultic practices:

Look, you serve your own interest on your fast day,

and oppress all your workers.

Look, you fast only to quarrel and to fight

and to strike with a wicked fist.

Such fasting as you do today will not make your voice heard on high.

Is such the fast that I choose,

a day to humble oneself?

Is it to bow down the head like a bulrush,

and to lie in sackcloth and ashes?

Will you call this a fast,

a day acceptable to the Lord?

Is not this the fast that I choose:

to loose the bonds of injustice,

to undo the thong of the yoke,

to let the oppressed go free,

and to break every yoke?

Is it not to share your bread with the hungry,

and bring the homeless poor into your house;

when you see the naked, to cover them,

And not to hide yourself your own kin?

(Isaiah 58:3b–7)

With the support of the Persian Empire, the priestly group eliminated any threat to its control, either from the prophetic group or from priests not from the line of the preexilic high priest Zadok. The Levites, for example, lost their priestly status at this time and were eventually relegated to temple functionaries. Ezra and Nehemiah, as agents of the Persian Empire, finalized this triumph through the reestablishment of the law and the rebuilding of the walls in the mid- to late fifth century BCE. The Zadokite priestly faction was now firmly in control.

Over time, the prophetic/visionary group lost all hope that their vision could be realized within history. Out of this desperate disillusionment, they began to focus more on the action of God beyond history and on a time of final judgment when God would punish those who had strayed from God's ways and redeem the faithful. This movement away from the historical grounding that had always been basic to the prophetic witness led eventually to the development of an apocalyptic understanding that emerged more fully in later centuries.

The battle between the priestly and prophetic camps was between two radically different religious orientations, both seeking a right relationship with God but conceiving the means to that right relationship in profoundly different ways. It was, in the words of Paul Hanson, a "contrast between two religious stances, the one centered around the formal worship of the temple, the other based on an attitude of humility and fear before Yahweh."[5]

## SOME POSSIBLE IMPLICATIONS

What intrigues me here, and offers significant insight for us in our time, is the striking contrast between these two religious stances that goes even further than the difference Hanson describes in the above quote. It is also a contrast of one seeking to maintain the status quo, the other to establish something new; one devoted to cultic worship, the other to justice and righteousness; one dependent on clergy, the other seeing everyone as a priest; one inwardly focused, the other outwardly; one concerned with piety, the other with the poor; one seeking to rebuild/renew/redevelop itself, the other to redeem the world; one focused on the institution, the other on the work of God in the world.

All of these differences leave us with a basic question that is not easy to answer, but is essential to our search for what it means to be faithful in today's world: Is God calling us today to rebuild, revitalize, and redevelop the existing and traditional structures of religion, or is God calling us to discern and participate in a new thing God is doing? There are perhaps those who say we need to do both. There is some measure of wisdom in that. I am always suspicious of either/or dichotomies that force us to choose one or the other. To be honest, however, my experience has been that all too often having it both ways is a means of having it my way. It allows us to choose the option we like and serves as a rationale for avoiding the difficult option or the possibility of a paradox that includes both and might lead us to a deeper truth.

I, of course, have a bias in all of this. I believe that given a choice between a priestly or prophetic approach to faith today, there is compelling reason to choose the prophetic. I believe as a church and congregations we are too concerned about institutional maintenance. I believe the focus on congregational renewal, revitalization, and redevelopment, although highly appropriate in some cases, is undermining our ability to develop a deeper understanding of God's work among us. I believe all of us have an uncanny ability to cloak whatever it is we want in an abundance of piety. We all too easily fall into believing that if we call a decision to do what we want to do discernment that's what it really is, if we say we are missional that's what we really are, if we pray about something we are really listening for what God is saying to us. I believe the existing structures of religion, be they congregations, denominations, or seminaries, place a high premium on their own survival. This is natural and to be expected for this is what institutions are supposed to do. It is essential for us to consistently ask ourselves, however, the question that the experience of the Return raises: Is this focus on institutional maintenance and survival pursued to the detriment of God's mission in the world?

Simply put: I believe this is a time to act more like prophets than priests, to adhere more to the program of the prophetic visionaries and the future they believed God had in store than to those who saw the work of God in the redevelopment of institutions, to trust more in God than in ourselves, to be willing to let go of what has been in order to embrace a new thing that God is doing. What happened 2,500 years ago in Jerusalem provides an interesting and challenging perspective for us today.

# 3

# BUT WAIT! THERE'S MORE!

I didn't come to the conclusions I made in the previous chapter solely because of my reading of this one period of biblical history. There is much more that supports the notion that now is the time to move on to a new thing.

## SECULAR WRITERS AND WHAT THEY SAY ABOUT CONTEMPORARY INSTITUTIONS

Robert Quinn, a professor in the business school of the University of Michigan, maintains that given the tumultuous nature of the world in which we live, deep change is essential. He contends that every institution today faces a fundamental choice between deep change and slow death. Deep change is his version of "the new thing." It is "major in scope, discontinuous with the past and generally irreversible."[1] He maintains this kind of change doesn't come from strategic plans. Rather, it arises out of a transforming spirit that shapes everything the organization is about. Further, it comes most often as a challenge to those who have held positions of power and influence. He refers to this group as the dominant coalition. Members of the dominant coalition may have helped the institution survive difficult times. They are undoubtedly loyal to it and even love it. Most often, they also believe deeply in what the institution has been about and resist, perhaps even deny the need for, significant change, seeing it as a threat to what is sacred. Tweaking may be needed, they admit, but not deep change. This belief on the part of those in power means, of course, that deep change most often comes from the fringes, not the center of an organization. It is propelled by outsiders, not insiders. Given this understanding of insiders and outsiders, it is interesting to view the priestly group as a dominant coalition, those who saw no great need to change and who therefore sought to maintain the status quo, who relied on their plans and themselves to do whatever needed to be done and, of course, to maintain their own position and power. The visionary group, on the other hand, can be viewed as the outsiders, those without formal authority, who saw things differently and had no particular attachment to the traditional structures, thus making them more attentive to a different way of seeing and doing.

The distinction between technical issues and adaptive challenges first described by Ronald Heifetz, who is a professor in the Kennedy School of Government at Harvard University, also provides a perspective on both the return from Babylonian captivity and our current situation. In Heifetz's view, a technical issue is one in which the problem and the solution are both known, so it is possible to rely on one's self or an "expert" to resolve the issue. Adaptive challenges, on the other hand, are those for which the solution and perhaps even the problem are unknown. Meeting an adaptive challenge always requires those involved to learn new ways of thinking and doing. Because of the defeat and destruction of Jerusalem, the situation those who returned from Exile faced was an adaptive challenge, requiring new learning. The priestly group's strategy of reinstituting the old structures and offices was an attempt to meet that adaptive challenge with a technical fix, which never provides a possibility of new learning because it relies on old knowledge and ways. The strategy of the visionary group, on the other hand, required new learning, as it invited the people into a new way of thinking about what God was asking of them. They also didn't provide specific answers to the question of what that meant, leaving it to the people to work out the details as learning took place. It was an attempt to meet the adaptive challenge presented by the Return.

Heifetz's presentation of adaptive challenges also provides insight for the time in which we live. Given the rapid and radical change that we are experiencing, adaptive challenges are likely to be more common than technical problems. In a time such as this the old answers rarely work; new answers need to be found. For this reason we would do well to question the strategy of the priestly group and consider that of the prophetic group. Ultimately, however, contemporary versions of both groups need to be involved in meeting the adaptive challenge. Heifetz is clear that the solution to an adaptive challenge involves a conflict of values and those holding the different values need to be engaged in the process. The battles of the fifth century BCE were so divisive that serious engagement of opposing sides was impossible. Today's political climate provides further evidence of the difficulty of maintaining engagement when the conflict of values is great. The involvement of those holding different values remains, however, an essential part of the process of meaningful change.

## RELIGIOUS WRITERS AND WHAT THEY SAY ABOUT THE CHURCH

Helpful perspectives that support the notion of the need for a "new thing" also appear in writing about the contemporary religious scene. Phyllis Tickle, in her book *The Great Emergence*, uses the image of a rummage sale to describe our current situation.[2] Every five hundred years, she says, the church has to have a rummage sale. The changes in the world have been so significant that the traditions that long held the church together and enabled people to keep the faith are no longer meaningful. The church needs to sort through all that it has accumulated in the way of structure, practice, theology, and language to decide what to keep and what to get rid of in order to minister faithfully and effectively, in order to be the church for the new time in which it finds itself. Tickle believes that we live in such a time. That is why ministerial leadership today is so difficult, why answers are hard to come by, why hard work is not producing the results we are accustomed to, why tension and blame abound.

If we work our way backward in the history of the faith, we discover that this need for a rummage sale happens just about every five hundred years. Five hundred years ago the rummage sale occurred during the Reformation. Five hundred years before that it was during the split between Eastern and Western Christianity. Five hundred years before that it was during the development of the monastery as a way to contend with the collapse of the Roman Empire with which the church had so closely identified itself. Five hundred years before that it was during the emergence of Christianity and the synagogue within Judaism when the temple was destroyed. Five hundred years before that (not surprisingly!) it was during the Exile and the Return. And five hundred years before that it was during the establishment of the kingship in Israel. In each of these times common understandings and ways of looking at the world had become out of sync with reality, common ground had disappeared. So it was a time of upheaval and change, of the disintegration of old patterns, ways of being and institutions.

In her more recent book, *Emergence Christianity,* Tickle describes our current situation this way: "Intellectually, politically, economically, culturally, sociologically, religiously, psychologically—every part of us and of how we are and how we live has, to some greater or lesser degree, been reconfiguring over the last century and a half, and those changes are now becoming a genuine maelstrom around us."[3] The sorting, deciding, saving, and unloading the rummage sale involves is a lot to deal with. No wonder we feel overwhelmed at times.

The good news in all of this, according to Tickle, is that each time we undergo one of these traumatic times of change three things happen: "(1) a new, more vital form of Christianity emerges, (2) the traditional organized expression of Christianity that had been dominant is reconstituted into a more pure, less ossified expression of its former self and (3) the faith is spread into new geographic and demographic areas."[4]

Another analysis of our current situation is more specifically American. Drawing on the work of historian William McLoughlin, Diana

Butler Bass, in her book *Christianity after Religion*, looks at religious awakenings and their relationship to social reform.[5] Awakenings, she contends, provide the occasion for cultural revitalization, which results in institutional restructuring and a redefinition of social goals. There have been four such awakenings in the history of the United States. The first, 1730–1760, was instrumental in the movement toward the Revolutionary War, the end of denominational dependence on European structures, and the development of more democratic forms of governance. The second, 1800–1830, grew out of some of the same forces that also resulted in the Civil War and led to the end of Calvinist dominance in Protestant theology. The third, 1890–1920, contended with the issues raised by industrialization and led to two different theological responses, the social gospel and Pentecostalism. It is our lot to be living in the midst of a fourth awakening, and like those who lived through the previous ones we will need to contend with conflict and dislocation, with turmoil and uncertainty. Out of it will come, however, a new way of being spiritual and religious that is more attuned to the time in which we live.

A somewhat different perspective is offered by Gerhard Von Rad in his book *The Message of the Prophets*, which is a revision of a section of his *Old Testament Theology*. Von Rad's discussion of the conditions of the times in which prophets appeared identifies some striking similarities with today and suggests the need for a prophetic word in our time. Let's look at each of these four conditions and draw some parallels to what we are experiencing today.

The years of the prophets were, Von Rad notes, a time of "degeneracy of Yahwism because of syncretism."[6] Israel's religion had been greatly influenced by other religions, losing its uniqueness and understanding of the way in which God was at work through them. Today, nationalism, militarism, patriotism, materialism, consumerism, or countless other "isms" have had a profound impact on Christianity. Today there is allegiance to a civil religion that is both influenced by Christianity and uses Christianity for its own purposes. There is a prosperity gospel cloaking financial avarice in pietistic platitudes. There is an all but automatic assumption that God is on our side in our wars and other military actions, coupled with strong attacks from people both within and outside of churches if anyone raises questions about the rightness and righteousness of what we are about in those wars and military actions. All of these are evidence of a syncretism in which it is virtually impossible to sort out faith from social conventions, national commitments, and economic convictions.

Prophets appeared in the past when through Israel's actions to arm itself and build alliances to ensure its security there was a "systematic emancipation from Yahweh and his offer of protection."[7] No longer having a sense of being guided by Yahweh, Israel became more and more dependent on its own power and wisdom, on what it could do on its own. Israel no longer needed God. People believed there was no longer a need to listen to God. Our knowledge, our technology, our skills, our planning all speak of a confidence in ourselves to know and to do what needs to be done all on our own. We can rely on a system of trickle-down economics to take care of issues of justice. We can trust in our technological advances to handle whatever environmental problems develop from our abuse of creation. We can depend on medical advances to prolong life. We can rely on organized sports to provide meaning and purpose for our children. We can do it all.

The times of the prophets were times in which the policies of "the state with its taxation and its civil service had brought about a further disintegration of the old social order within the tribes of Israel."[8] Great landowners who lived in towns controlled the economy. Peasants became less and less free. Ownership of land became more and more centralized in the hands of a few. Economic disparity increased and with it social injustice. Today, we deal with banks and corporations that are deemed too big to fail, tax breaks for the rich and reduced support for feeding the hungry, elections that can ever more easily be bought with big money, growing disparity between rich and poor, and the decline of the middle class.

The times of the prophets were times in which the ever-changing balances of power among nations brought about "a shift in political power in the realm of general history."[9] A dizzying array of nations came to power, conquered land, lost power, lost lands. In times when the ability of external powers to control events in Israel was waning, Israel could assert a measure of independence, but lost it as soon as a new power appeared on the scene. Today the rise of terrorism; the inability of any nation (including the most powerful nation in the world) to assert its will on others, to bring peace, to spread democracy; and all the disastrous consequences of attempts to do these things create an instability that leads to fear and the loss of hope, to anger and the desire to strike out.

If a prophetic word was needed in such ancient times, it is also needed today.

## SOME POSSIBLE IMPLICATIONS

We have covered much ground in our attempt to gain an understanding of the broader context in which we live and make decisions about the future of the church in general and our own congregations in particular. I have, of necessity, been selective in the perspectives I chose to explore and from which I hope we can gain insight.

While I am not one who believes that history repeats itself, I do believe we can gain insight for these days from reflecting on earlier days and perhaps even drawing some parallels between that time and our own, provided, as Walter Brueggemann has suggested, we use them as metaphors, not maps. The time of the Return can be used in this way, for there are significant parallels to be drawn.

The priestly understanding of the need for cultic purity is still with us and exercises significant influence. We can see it in the desire to "put prayer back in public schools." Those who advocate for this view claim that the social and cultural ills of the present can only be addressed through the reestablishment of this cultic practice of civil religion. Also, the theological affirmation that the church is that place where "the Word is rightly preached and the sacraments properly administered" is a priestly claim that defines church primarily from the perspective of its cultic practices, not its mission. And in like manner, the rather significant emphasis that many congregations place on (and the considerable amount of money that is used for) the maintenance of church buildings speaks not only of the importance of place in our meaning making and the practical need for space, but also has significant parallels to Israel's compelling need to rebuild the temple.

As I consider these and other common features between that time and this, I am led to make several affirmations of the world in which we live and the church's response to it as we attempt to be faithful.

This is a time in which rebuilding (renewing, revitalizing, redeveloping) old institutions will not be enough and in many cases probably will not work.

This is a time in which old institutions, old structures, old ways will need to die.

This is a time in which we need to be highly attentive to the new thing God is doing in our midst.

This is a time in which we need to face the difficult, often painful reality that new life comes only when we die to the old life. Too many renewal efforts seek to avoid this practical and theological reality, and because they do so, they are unable to address the true nature of our situation and offer a solid hope for the future. We need to be more concerned about resurrection than renewal.

In such a time as this we need to remind ourselves that God is not primarily concerned with institutional maintenance or even survival. And we need to be open to the possibility that this applies to us and to the institutions to which we have devoted our lives and which in many ways sustain us still—institutions that we love. Although another five hundred years passed before the temple was destroyed in 70 CE, it was not rebuilt. If we need evidence that God is not primarily a maintainer of institutions we need look no further than that. So in this time when so much is up for grabs we would be well to remind ourselves that institutions, whether they be local congregations or national denominations, are not what matter most.

In such a time as this, we need to set aside many, if not most, of the standards by which we have determined our success or failure, our effectiveness or lack thereof. Baptisms, membership, budgets—any and all forms of statistical analysis—don't tell us what we most need to know about the church and what it is about in these days.

In such a time as this, we need to disabuse ourselves of any notion that we have the answer or even that we will discover the answer and instead seek to open ourselves to the presence and experience of God in our lives and in the world.

None of the affirmations I have shared is easy to implement in our lives. In fact, some of them may be impossible for me and for you. That's not the point. What matters is that we are convinced that God is up to something in this time, as much as in any time the Bible talks about, any time in history. What matters is that we are determined to be part of that thing, no matter what it is.

## A WORD ABOUT THE REIGN OF GOD

I have to admit that I am deeply troubled by what happened to the prophetic/visionary group as the priestly group gained control and reestablished the old ways of religion. As I noted in the last chapter, the triumph of the priestly group in the reestablishment of the temple led to a loss of hope that those things they held dear would ever become reality. When they lost hope they also lost the historical grounding for their faith that had been a vital part of the prophetic witness. They were left with nothing but an apocalyptic vision that sometime in the future God would do something. And with that, they lost any reason to be about God's work in the present. I don't want that to happen to me or to you, which led me to wonder what would make it possible for me to be more like one of those classical prophets, grounded in the present reality even when it was dismal, but still hopeful about the future. The answer I came to, the one that works for me, is found in the concept of the reign of God, the belief that it is both already with us and at the same time not yet fully present. This belief grounds us in history, but doesn't make us dependent upon history. It allows us to be about the work God calls us to do, no matter how difficult or even useless it may seem at the time. It is possible to always be hopeful even when there seems to be no reason at all, because our ultimate hope is rooted in the future that God will most certainly provide. If that is our source of hope, the realities of this time, this world, this history will not disillusion us. We may not be optimistic, but we need not be without hope.

# Part 2

# Old and New Questions

# PART 2 INTRODUCTION

**M**ax Depree says, "The first responsibility of a leader is to define reality."[1] He means by that, I think, that there needs to be a common understanding of the context in which any group or organization is operating. It is the responsibility of the leader to develop that understanding in a way that reflects the actual reality of the context as much as possible.

People's understanding of reality is shaped, by and large, by assumptions they make. No one can grasp the entirety of reality, so we make assumptions to get a handle on things. We all do. We couldn't live if we didn't. If every experience were new, fresh, without context we would be overwhelmed and unable to function. Assumptions allow us to fit experiences into a context, make sense out of them, and respond to them. They are essential—and yet, they can also be the cause of an incredible amount of trouble. Continuing to make assumptions that are no longer viable because they are not grounded in the way things are can lead to our digging ourselves into ever-deepening holes from which it becomes increasingly difficult to escape. One of the functions of leadership involves examining what Robert Kegan and Lisa Laskow Lahey in their books *How the Way We Talk Can Change the Way We Work* and *Immunity to Change* call "big assumptions."[2] These assumptions are so deeply embedded in our minds and the way we do things that no one even thinks about them. We just continue to use them to make sense out of what happens to us and to determine how we will respond. The assumptions we make about the way the world is and what the church should do lead to questions we ask that shape our planning. We ask: "How can we do this particular thing?" without first asking if "this particular thing" is really the thing a church should be doing. We have just assumed that it is.

When our assumptions are unexamined, they continue to shape the questions we ask and make it difficult to ask new ones. If those assumptions are no longer valid, the questions we ask are no longer helpful. Edwin Friedman notes that one of the problems of the world today is that we continually seek new answers to the same old questions rather than asking new questions: "In the search for the solution to any problem, questions are always more important than answers because the way one frames the question, or the problem, already predetermines the range of answers one can conceive in response."[3]

When we talk about the need for church to face and meet adaptive challenges as we did in chapter 3, we are talking about the need to think and act differently. That is the learning that we need to engage. Helping people ask different questions can be an early step in that learning process. We have passed the time when better answers to the old questions will do the job. We need new questions.

In the following chapters of this section I will offer some suggestions for old questions we need to put in what Phyllis Tickle refers to as the once-every-five-hundred-year rummage sale the church needs to have, along with some new questions we might begin to ask. It's not that the old questions weren't valid at one time or even that they have no place in the church today. Rather, the new questions, if they are the questions that form our approach to ministry, will lead us to new insights and new learning.

I am not seeking to provide the answers in these pages. The truth is, meaningful answers can only come from people in congregations as they engage the questions in their own particular context. I'll share some notions about why these are questions we should be asking and how we might engage them, but I'll leave the rest to you. In fact, what I really want to do is to invite you to live with the new questions for a while, because I believe that in living with them new ways of being and doing church will emerge. The familiar line from the poet Rainer Maria Rilke can guide us: "Live the questions now. Perhaps you will then gradually, without noticing it, one distant day live right into the answer."[4]

Be assured, I am not saying that if you ask these questions you'll find the way to renew, revitalize, or redevelop your church. It may happen. But you may just as likely discover that asking these questions takes you down a road to some other alternative that you hadn't thought of before. What I feel pretty confident about, however, is that asking these new questions will bring us closer to discovering what God is seeking from us in this time. I also believe asking these new questions will help ensure that whatever the future holds for us and our congregations we will be more faithful in the work we are about right now. And that is a pretty wondrous thing!

# 4

# IN/OUT

*Old Question: "How do we bring them in?"*
*New Question: "How do we send them out?"*

Of all the Big Assumptions most congregations make about their life and ministry, this might be the biggest. It probably has the most significant impact on a congregation, and, as such, is the one we will explore most closely.

Virtually everyone assumes that one of the purposes of the church, if not the main purpose, is to bring in new members. It is so basic to most thinking about the church that it may not even be stated, perhaps not even conscious. It is an assumption that is just accepted as *truth*. It is variously understood as making certain that people are saved and won't go to hell, providing a community for spiritual growth, offering a means for dealing with the stresses and strains of life, and any number of other interpretations. All of them, however, are about getting people into the church. It may not always be possible, but to whatever extent it is, churches should be doing it. Consultants and workshop leaders provide strategies for doing it. Denominations tell wondrous stories of churches that have succeeded in doing it. Pastors who do it are usually deemed more successful than those who don't do it and typically have better chances of moving on to larger, more prestigious congregations as they climb the ministerial career ladder. It's the question that fueled the church-growth movement and the interest in worship evangelism. It's the standard used by many to determine the vitality of a congregation and the viability of a denomination. And it is the cause of the great angst we have regarding "the decline of the Protestant mainline." All of this is based in the assumption that bringing people in is what churches are supposed to do.

The notion behind the bring-them-in assumption is that the institutional church is the place everyone can and should be, that we in the church have something they need and can't get anyplace else, and because of that it is the place God wants everyone to be. This is the impulse that drives the belief that a major responsibility of those who are already in a church (and if not everyone, then certainly the pastor) is bringing others in. This is what evangelism is all about. It is at the very heart of what it means to be a church. The formative question for most congregations has been and remains, "How do we bring them in?"

Answering this question has spawned an industry of workshops, resources, consultants, products, and gimmicks. Staid mainline congregations that rejected many of the notions of the church-growth movement because it was too evangelistic for them still assume that growth is an appropriate criterion for determining success and viability. They keep statistics, carefully measuring the growth or decline of congregational, judicatory, and national organizations. As an example, the Unitarian Universalist Association, like many more liberal denominations not noted for their evangelistic fervor, has its Breakthrough Congregations initiative:

> [The initiative is] an effort to identify those congregations that had achieved *significant and sustained* numerical growth and give them an opportunity to share at General Assembly what they've done, and how they've done it. Why not look to the experts—those lay and professional leaders who have already "cracked the nut" around growth and give them the opportunity at general assembly to share their wisdom?[1]

Denominational resources, conversations among pastors, and continuing education offerings (sometimes blatantly, sometimes subtly) are constructed to answer this question.

The assumption that this is the primary purpose of the church, however, is little more than a vestige of the days of high Christendom, when there was only one Church in the West and everyone was born into a parish. This provided the common experience of faith that was deemed essential to the well-being of society and the stability of the state. At that time there was no need to "bring them in" in a church-growth sense, because they were already in, at least in theory. The bring-them-in effort in those days was restricted to converting those considered heathen, usually in foreign lands. Over time, however, church membership became less and less universal and growing numbers of people were not members. Still, the image of everyone belonging to a church remained a powerful force feeding a desire among church leaders at least to bring those outside into the fold.

Theologically, the bring-them-in assumption has its roots in the premise that outside the church there is no salvation. While many people wouldn't be quite so blatant about it and some cringe whenever it is said, it is still the belief that lurks behind the desire to bring people into the church. The church (and only the church) has what is needed to bring healing and wholeness. Outside the church this cannot happen, so bringing people in is our Christian responsibility, allowing others to experience what we already have.

Emotionally, the assumption has its roots in the good old days when churches were full and were seen as significant players in community life because anyone who was anyone belonged. In many ways this emotionality may be the most powerful motivator. It's about nostalgia based in a sense of loss: The choir just isn't as big as it used to be. The staff is smaller than it used to be. The sanctuary is no longer filled to capacity on Christmas Eve. We just don't have that great sense of the Spirit's presence that used to come from filling the sanctuary with song when we sang the old hymns. The community leaders are no longer members and in fact barely acknowledge that the church exists, scheduling all sorts of events that conflict with worship.

Financially, the bring-them-in assumption has its roots in an ever-increasing need for more people to underwrite the budget. It is a survival strategy seized on by both congregations and denominations that see the downward trend in membership and giving. Smaller congregations are willing to sacrifice the coziness of a community in which everyone knows everyone else in order to ensure a more secure financial base. Larger congregations seek ways to continue supporting their large staffs. It isn't pretty. In fact, it's embarrassing enough that many church members deny that it's true, but it is real and often drives the desire to bring more people into the church. It is one of those hard realities we need to recognize.

If anyone doubts the way in which this bring-them-in assumption is at play in church life, all they need do is listen to the response the next time someone—be it church member, pastor, denominational official, or church consultant—rattles off a bunch of statistics that demonstrate congregations and denominations are getting smaller. Virtually everyone will sit there, absorbing and bemoaning the reality that the data point to and assuming that it is a problem in desperate need of a remedy, if not evidence of a dismal failure on the part of churches to fulfill the purpose that God has given them. No one will question the underlying assumption that leads to these conclusions, because virtually everyone accepts it, even if it remains unspoken.

But, in the post-Christendom world, the assumption that the purpose of the church is to bring in new members is up for grabs. Let me be clear: it is not wrong for a congregation to grow. I am not opposed to people joining a church. But this can no longer be the criterion for determining whether a congregation is faithfully responding to God's call to be the church; it can no longer be the formative question that motivates what congregations do. Congregation as parish is dead. In a diverse, anti-institutional and secular world it simply doesn't make sense for the primary operating assumption of the church to be getting people to become members. Congregation as mission station and congregation as disciple-forming community are more appropriate images for us today. They each provide a new way of being for the church. Getting new members is not what matters most. What matters is how those who are already there are being equipped and embolden to bring God's love to the world. Growth may well be a byproduct, but it cannot be the purpose.

## SOME POSSIBLE MODELS

There is no one way to be a congregation in which "How do we send them out?" is the formative question. The way that works depends on the particular situation in which you find yourself and a vast number of variables: the people, the gifts they have, the church's history, the community, the passions, the leadership, the fear, the hope, the determination, the conflict, the joy, the grief. All of these and many more factors shape the congregation as it sets its course for the future. The answers to this question will only come through careful reflection, prayerful discernment, and trial and error. It is helpful, however, to have some possible models in mind, not to copy, but to stimulate thought, discussion, and prayer. We'll take a look at three of those now.

In *Kicking Habits*, Tom Bandy presents models for two types of churches. One he calls The Declining Church System, the other The Thriving Church System.[2] In truth no church is completely one or the other. It's not possible to divide churches up into just two categories and designate them as either declining or thriving. Bandy's types, however, reinforce much of what I have said in this chapter. Bandy describes a core process for each type of church—what each type sets out to do with those who are involved.

In Bandy's Declining Church System, which we might call the Bring-Them-In System, the core process is: enrolled, informed, nominated, supervised, and kept. Those who are involved are *enrolled* and have their names placed on the official membership rolls, usually quite soon after they begin to participate in the life of the congregation. As they become further involved they are *informed* about the history, polity, and beliefs of the church, learning about both the people and the organization. Once they are sufficiently informed they can be *nominated* to serve on a board or committee of the church, often placed in the more difficult-to-fill and less influential positions first. As they serve in these positions they continue to be *supervised* in order to ensure that they handle the responsibilities of their position appropriately and to determine whether they can properly handle greater responsibilities in more influential positions. All of this is done with the intention that those who go through this process are *kept*, so that the institutional structure of the church can be maintained, the programs of the church delivered, and the financial viability of the church preserved.

In contrast, the core process in Bandy's Thriving Church System, which we might call the Send-Them-Out System is: changed, gifted, called, equipped, and sent. People become invested in the life of a congregation because they have been *changed*. Something has happened in their lives to convince them that they cannot continue as before. Perhaps a trauma called into question the way they had put their lives together and they have a sense that life will be different if they are aware of God's presence and leading. Or perhaps through participation in the ministry or mission of the church they discovered a new vitality to life, a new reason for living, and they want to experience that more fully. Either way, change that has taken place in their lives has brought them to the church. As they become further involved in the life of the congregation they begin to realize that they are *gifted* people, that God has given them gifts that make them the unique people they are. But because this church is focused on ministry, they also discover that having gifts means little if these gifts are not used in some way to make the reign of God more fully present. So they discover that they are *called* to serve the world in a way that uses their gifts. Ministry, however, isn't a simple thing, so those who discern their gifts and call also need to be *equipped* to minister faithfully and effectively. All this is done so that they can be *sent* into the world to share in the work of God, or as Ephesians puts it, to do the good works, "which God prepared beforehand to be our way of life" (Ephesians 2:10).

Another possible model for being a send-them-out congregation is the missional church. Much of the theoretical underpinnings for this model can be found in the work of The Gospel and Our Culture Network, which has focused on a concern for being the church in a post-Christendom world. Recognizing the demise of the Age of Christendom, in which the church could count on significant cultural support for its work, beliefs, and practices, those involved in the network began to explore a new understanding of what it means to be church. Darrel Gruder, one of the leaders of the network, explains the situation this way: "This is a time for a dramatically new vision. The current predicament of churches in North America requires more than a mere tinkering with long-assumed notions about the identity and mission of the church. Instead, . . . there is a need for reinventing or rediscovering the church in this new kind of world."[3]

A central feature of this reinventing is a rethinking of the concept of the reign of God, which was central to the teaching and ministry of Jesus. Traditionally this has been associated almost exclusively with the church: the reign of God is present in the church. Writing in *The Missional Church*, George Hunsburger, also a member of the Gospel and Our Culture Network, notes that this view leads to the belief that "church extension or church growth is the equivalent of kingdom extension or kingdom growth and the reign of God is coterminous with the people who embrace it through faith and gather together as the church. This view leads easily to the affirmation that there is no salvation outside the church."[4] However, Hunsburger argues that the reign of God is not about the church, but the world. That is where God is present and at work to bring peace and justice, healing and wholeness to all creation. If the reign of God is about all creation, not just the church, mission is rooted in the work God is doing in the world. The church exists to further that work. This means "the church of Jesus Christ is not the purpose or goal of the gospel, but rather its instrument and witness."[5] In other words, the purpose of the church is not to build the church, but to do God's work in the world. This purpose leads the church into a world whose values and practices are often at odds with the gospel to participate in that work. It is not about bringing them in, but sending them out.

A third model for a send-them-out congregation is the disciple-forming community. This model utilizes the concept of discipleship annunciated in the Great Commission.

As you go into the world, make disciples of all kinds of people, immerse them in the presence of the Father, Son and Holy Spirit, and

show them how to do everything I have commanded you. Remember: I
am with you until that day when the job is done.[6]

The assumption is that those in the church are already going into the
world. They are to go in a way that is different from most, however,
because they go to show people how to do the things that Jesus commanded them to do. This means, first and foremost, that they themselves
need to live as Jesus has commanded them to live. That is the only way
they can show others how to do it. Dallas Willard describes it this way:

> Now, some might be shocked to hear that what the church really needs
> is not more people, more money, better buildings or programs, more
> education, or more prestige. Christ's gathered people, the church, has
> always been at its best when it had little or none of these. All it needs
> to fulfill Christ's purposes on earth is *the quality of life he makes real
> in the life of his disciples.* Given that quality, the church will prosper
> from everything that comes its way as it makes clear and available on
> earth the "life that is life indeed."[7]

Willard goes on to describe the challenge facing the disciple-forming
congregation:

> So the greatest issue facing the world today, with all its heartbreaking
> needs, is whether those who, by profession or culture, are identified as
> "Christians" will become disciples—students, apprentices, practition-
> ers—*of Jesus Christ,* steadily learning from him how to live the life of
> the Kingdom . . . into every corner of human existence. Will they break
> out of the churches to be his Church—to be, without human force or
> violence, his mighty force for good on earth, drawing the churches
> after them toward the eternal purposes of God?[8]

This way of faith is about breaking out of churches, not bringing others
into them. It's about living the life of the Kingdom, not maintaining an
institution.

The church that is a disciple-forming community focuses on those
who are already there, offering them experiences through which they can
deepen their relationships with God, with themselves, and with others in

community. It seeks to equip them by providing experiences through which they can discern their gifts and the call that comes to them to use those gifts and grow in the knowledge and skills they need to serve God in today's world. It provides experiences of ministry through which they encounter and respond to the needs of the world so that God's reign may become more fully present. All this is done so that they can go into the world to share God's love. They may do this on their own, at work, in their families and communities; they may do it with others in ministries developed by the congregation. The key is they are going out.[9]

## SOME POSSIBLE IMPLICATIONS

As we will see with all the other questions, everything the congregation does changes when the question is different. If we frame what we are about in congregations by asking a different key question—not "How do we bring them in?" but "How do we send them out?"—everything, from worship to mission to education to structure, changes. Again, what actually happens depends on the particular setting, but here are some possible implications for you to consider.

*Congregations may see the purpose of worship not as attracting new members, but as inspiring current ones to live more fully and faithfully in the world.* Worship is no longer seen primarily as evangelism. Making a worship service entertaining and removing traditional symbols and language so outsiders will feel more comfortable is no longer a concern. Being seeker-sensitive is not the aim of worship planning. What matters most is the way worship nourishes, strengthens, and emboldens those who are there, so they can move out into God's work in the world. In order to do that, worship does consider the lives, events, hurts, and hopes of the world or it won't lead people into the world. Worship cannot consistently avoid the issues that impact the lives of people and events in the world. But it cannot be shaped by those issues or current cultural trappings. It needs to maintain a clear focus on God and praising God, for in the final analysis that is what nourishes, strengthens, and emboldens people for service in the world. Whether a congregation follows a traditional liturgy or crafts a contemporary service, the purpose of worship is forming more faithful disciples. Everything is different because the formative question is no longer about bringing those who aren't involved in from the world, but sending those who are involved out into the world.

*A congregation may see mission in a different perspective.* With this new formative question, mission is no longer exclusively seen just as projects the congregation adopts and does collectively. In fact, it is not about projects at all, but a way of being, a way of living in the world. Mission is about how each person lives in the normal routines of his or her daily life. Certainly there is still a need for collective mission efforts initiated by a congregation. But mission will also be about the way we move out into the world as individuals who engage all the involvements of our lives with a sense of ministry and mission, of sharing God's love. Mission might be the care given by a parent for her or his children, the work of an executive in the office, a visit to a local bar to talk with those who are lonely. At home, at work, in the community, we are at work furthering the reign of God, sharing God's love, doing the good deeds God has prepared for us to do. All this is part of the mission of the church.

*Congregations may begin to believe that education is not so much a matter of learning the right answers as living the faithful life.* Content is still important. Knowing the Bible, being familiar with core theological concepts and how they bring insight and meaning to our lives, remain vitally important. But at its core we learn to live as people of faith in the world through an enculturation process in which we develop a way of seeing and being that enables us to follow Jesus more fully in our lives and be more fully engaged in God's mission in the world. The purpose of education is transformation, not formation.

*Pastoral care may not only address the healing of people but nurture them in their lives as disciples.* A church that focuses on sending out understands that everyone has a ministry. We sometimes think those in need of pastoral care are being ministered to, but not ministering themselves, because they are too overwhelmed by whatever it is they are dealing with to care for others. If we recognize that they, as all disciples, have a ministry, this puts pastoral care in a different perspective. We are not just caring for them; we are also nurturing them and equipping them. We are encouraging them to discover the truth of the biblical insight that true healing and wholeness come when we look beyond ourselves and seek to serve others. The way this movement is accomplished varies greatly, of course, depending on the particular situation, but this understanding expands the purpose of pastoral care.

*The old institutional structure that focused on involving as many people as possible may need to be dismantled, freeing people to be sent rather than kept.* Large committees, oversight boards, and representative councils all provided places for people to be involved in the institutional life of the congregation. Most churches have discovered that it is no longer possible to maintain this structure. So, when denominational polity permits, the bylaws are changed to reduce the number of people on boards and shorten the length of terms. While perhaps a step in the right direction, in most congregations a more radical approach is needed to make the structure as lean as possible so that as few people as possible are needed to sustain it. When this is done more people are freed to be sent rather than kept.

The impetus behind each of these changes is asking a different question and then letting our exploration of that question lead us to think differently about the congregation, its purpose, and mission. Asking a new question won't guarantee anything—certainly not growth or a balanced budget. Just making "How do we send them out?" one of the formative questions, however, will increase the chances of the congregation aligning itself more closely with God's work in the world and helping to shape the future to which God is leading us.

# 5

# PASTOR/CONGREGATION

*Old Question: "What should the pastor do?"*
*New Question: "What is our congregation's shared ministry?"*

The classic division of labor in a congregation goes something like this:

It is the pastor's responsibility to take care of members and do ministry on their behalf. The pastor is to

- provide a meaningful, uplifting worship service,
- visit those who could not attend,
- care for the sick and troubled, and
- be involved in mission concerns in the name of the congregation— that is, take care of the needy people who come by the church, serve on boards of service organizations, and support good causes, as long as they are not controversial.

It is the responsibility of the laity to maintain the institution. They are to

- manage the building and the budget,
- ensure the continuance of the institution through the Sunday school and youth group so that there will be another generation to replace the current one,
- give,
- attend worship, and

- serve on boards and committees.

While we rarely see these roles in their pure form, this concept of divided responsibilities still operates in the thinking of a significant number of laity and clergy. It shapes their understanding of the roles each is to play in the congregation. And it supports the notion that operates in a number of churches that the pastor is a temporary hired hand who has responsibility for caring for us and doing good things on our behalf.

Coupled with this understanding of roles there is often a hierarchical understanding of the role of clergy. Pastors as designated holy ones are special, endowed with a certain power through education and ordination. Laity see them as somehow particularly tuned in to God and knowledgeable about God in a way that they can never be. They are able to live devout and holy lives and ponder the divine, relieving others, who have to face the harsh realities of the real world, from having to do so. They have a depth of understanding of the Bible and theology that is impossible for less-educated laity to achieve, giving clergy special authority in these matters. All of which leaves laity dependent upon clergy for the information they need to know about faith and for the various ministrations of the church, such as the sacraments and pastoral care.

Clergy usually support this understanding of roles and fulfill their responsibilities according to it, seeking to protect their prerogatives and powers (and, I might add, their pensions). They, often with the backing of their denomination's polity, restrict the performance of certain functions of the church to themselves and in a variety of ways seek to further a notion that they are mediators between God and the members of the congregation—whether through preaching, teaching, administering the sacraments, or other means. They do this in all sorts of subtle and not-so-subtle ways. For example, a pastor who leads the congregation in the sharing of celebrations and concerns before prayer, commenting on each concern and sharing additional information, making it clear that she or he already knows about this situation and is responding to it, provides evidence of a compassionate understanding of the needs and concerns of parishioners. But in doing this, she or he undercuts the notion that it is the community that provides care and reinforces the notion that the pastor is the primary care giver in the congregation.

Taken together these two views of the clergy/laity relationship—pastor as hired hand and pastor as designated holy one—enable congregations (and in some cases denominations) to create detailed descriptions of the role and responsibility of the pastor. Most congregations also have an array of noncontractual, often unspoken assumptions about what their pastor should do, many of which are intended to relieve members of the responsibility of growing in their own faith and ministry. It is the pastor's responsibility to be the primary purveyor of religious goods and services in the congregation. The pastor is to ensure that the Word is rightly preached and the sacraments properly administered. The pastor must work to provide a steady flow of new members, offer a continuing array of new program possibilities, keep everyone happy at all times, care for whomever is in need whenever that need arises, be engaged in caring ministries in the community and world, and make it happen—whatever the congregation's particular "it" might be. In actual practice, the classic division of labor is still very much present. It continues to support a mind-set that places primary responsibility on the pastor and discounts the role and responsibility of laity for their own growth in faith and ministry in the world. It is inwardly focused and clergy-centered, which undercuts the possibility of a congregation becoming a community of faith that uses the gifts of all for the work of God in the world. It diminishes the vitality of the congregation because it

- lessens the possibility that laity will see themselves as gifted for ministry;
- supports laity in denying their own responsibility for growth in life and faith;
- lessens the congregation's ability to involve everyone in meeting the adaptive challenges it faces;
- sets up an almost inevitable situation, especially in the context of decline, in which each party can blame the other for failure to fulfill their role rather than assume joint responsibility for the ministry of the congregation;

- encourages both clergy and laity to go through the motions of playing church rather than live faithfully as individuals and as a community.

The negative impact of continued adherence to these traditional roles of clergy and laity suggests the need to change the core question from "What should the pastor do?" to "What is our congregation's shared ministry?" The new question recognizes that pastor and people together are engaged in growing spiritually and living faithfully.

To get a better handle on the need for this change in questions it will be helpful to review a few historical developments and theological perspectives.

Alan Roxburgh, in his chapter "Missional Leadership: Equipping God's People for Mission" in *Missional Church*, offers a brief description of the evolving role of clergy in the church. In the early church, primary leadership rested in the apostles. Apostles were the people who not only had known Jesus but took on a primary role of bringing the gospel to the world. Apostolic leaders were leaders who were sent into the world to share the Good News about Jesus. By the third century, in response to a need to deal with a variety of heresies and to disciple converts, apostolic leaders had taken on a priestly role that focused on being repositories of correct knowledge that would protect the church and its members from heresy. That role continued to evolve as the church became a state church and the Age of Christendom took hold. Over time leadership in the church became based in "a priesthood of sacramental, holy orders in which the power of Christ's presence resided. . . . No longer a mission band of God's people, [the church] became a religious organization in which the means of grace were sacramentally communicated through an ordained priesthood and the reign of God identified with the church structures and its sacraments."[1]

The Reformation brought a change in the role of clergy that Roxburgh describes as a movement from priest to pedagogue. The role of the pastor as teacher took on greater importance and the sermon became the primary teaching tool. It became comparable in importance to the administration of the sacraments, which had been central in the liturgy of the church prior to that time.

The Enlightenment brought the next significant change in the role of clergy, which Roxburgh sees as the development of the professional. This view, which paralleled the development of professional training in other areas, promoted a clergy class devoted to acquiring knowledge and skills and engaging in the significant education this necessitated. In recent years three roles of clergy as professionals have come to the forefront: (1) counselor (responding to individual need), (2) manager (serving as the congregation's CEO), and (3) technician (defining and meeting the congregation's strategic goals). The view of pastor as professional led to the development of seminary-based education, which "remains firmly committed to the model of preparing a professional clergy for a set of tasks considered to be 'ministry.'"[2]

The understanding of the role of clergy that still operates in most congregations has a direct impact on the role of laity. Because it demands extensive preparation for involvement in ministry, it undercuts the role of laity in the life of the congregation and minimizes the way in which their gifts can be used within the Body. The priesthood of all believers remains an elusive goal, even in churches that honor the concept.[3]

In many places the priest, pedagogue, and professional models of the role of clergy are breaking down. What is important for our purposes, however, is to recognize and accept the continuing power they have in the thinking and practice of clergy, laity, and congregations. They lead to a significant number of assumptions about the church and the way it should function that we need to consider as candidates for the rummage sale.

The view of clergy as priest, pedagogue, and professional is being challenged by a number of postmodern, post-Christendom sensibilities. A suspicion of hierarchy, a desire for experience, a developing sense of the importance of spirituality, and the availability of a vast number of resources for spiritual growth outside the confines of the church all serve to reduce the influence clergy have in the lives of laity. These traditional roles no longer provide a basis for meaningful ministry. And yet, they have worked for so long they are deeply ingrained in both our thinking and acting. It is difficult even to be aware of the ways in which these roles shape our understanding of clergy, and by default laity. The error is not so much in maintaining the need for priests, pedagogues, and professionals, as in assigning those roles exclusively to clergy. Seeing clergy as the only ones who fulfill these roles is yet another vestige of Christendom; when everyone was a member of a parish, there was significant cultural support for the beliefs and practices of the faith, and most people were uneducated if not illiterate. Focusing on what happened within the church made sense then, as the laity relied on an educated leader to provide the religious services they needed. These roles fit nicely with the hierarchical and institutional nature of modernity and Christendom, providing an appropriate and important role for clergy in the life of the community. But Christendom is over. In the postmodern, post-Christendom world in which we live, with its suspicion of institutions, dislike of hierarchy, and desire for experience and involvement, clergy who seek to claim these roles as their exclusive domain are likely to be challenged by laity. Additionally, in a time when more and more congregations cannot afford full-time pastors it is essential that laity take on responsibilities that were at one time seen as the exclusive province of clergy. So, for example, many denominations are dealing today with the difficult task of determining what precisely will be required for one seeking "an alternative path to ordination," with "alternative" meaning without a seminary education.

One simple example illustrates the way in which these traditional clergy roles are no longer viable. Tony Jones, a leader in the emerging church movement, in his book *The Church Is Flat* points out the way in which the Internet radically changes the role of clergy as pedagogues. "Ready access to theological and biblical resources ha[s] at once both allowed church members to investigate their theological questions and also partially mitigated the need for seminary-trained pastors."[4] True, one cannot trust everything one reads on the Internet, but inquiring minds do have access to quality information that creates a different context for both teaching and preaching. Pronouncement becomes less viable, dialogue more appropriate. This is just one of the factors that lead to the democratization of roles, which in turn leads to a questioning of the need for clergy and the ordination that sets them apart.

The need for a change in roles of clergy and laity isn't just a matter of accommodating to a new cultural reality, however.

Biblically, there are any number of passages, most of which are quite familiar, that support an adjustment in the role of clergy and support for a shared ministry. In many cases this familiarity has led not to contempt, but to safe and shallow interpretation. Take Ephesians 4 as an example.

> But each of us was given grace according to the measure of Christ's gift. . . . The gifts he gave were that some would be apostles, some prophets, some evangelists, some pastors and teachers, to equip the saints for the work of ministry, for building up the body of Christ, until all of us come to the unity of the faith and of the knowledge of the Son of God, to maturity, to the measure of the full stature of Christ. (Ephesians 4:7, 11–13)

There are some pretty clear insights about both leadership and ministry here. The first is that leadership is to be shared; in the church there can never be a "solo" anything. A variety of gifts is given because a variety of gifts is needed for the body of Christ to function as it should. No one person has all the gifts, but they are all needed in the leadership of the church. The pastor/teacher is only one among several, but the way we most often structure leadership in the church and the way we practice ordination indicate we believe either that the person in this role does have all the gifts or that the other gifts are not needed. The pastor/teacher role may suffice for nurturing individuals in the faith and imparting knowledge about the faith, but more than this is essential for the leadership of the church to be faithful and effective. That's why other gifts are given. The implication is clear: if the gifts are given, they are to be used. Apostles, prophets, and evangelists are also needed to lead the church. And since no one person has all those gifts, some type of cooperative effort and structure is needed. One person cannot exercise all the gifts.

Second, this passage tells us something about the nature and purpose of the church's ministry. The gifts that are given to leaders are to be used "to equip the saints for the work of ministry." That means everyone has a ministry, everyone is involved in the ministry of the church. I am certain that hundreds of thousands, if not millions of sermons have been preached on this passage. Nearly all of them have extolled the importance of all believers being involved in ministry. Nearly all have encouraged, if not urged, laity to discover and claim their ministry, reminding them of the importance of Martin Luther's great insight about the ministry of the laity. I've given any number of sermons like that myself. But how often was it clear that this ministry is one that we all have in order to share God's love with others who are not part of the congregation? How often did these sermons lead to a deeper conviction that the ministry of all the saints is indeed the purpose of the church, the way in which the body of Christ was built up? How often did any of us make the leap to proclaiming that the participation of all the saints in ministry is the way, in fact the only way, we "come to the unity of the faith and of the knowledge of the Son of God, to maturity, to the measure of the full stature of Christ," as Ephesians tells us it does?

Theologically, the work of Jürgen Moltmann also speaks to the importance of changing the formative question to "What is our congregation's shared ministry?"[5] He has identified three paradigms for the church that have each come to the fore at different points in history.

First, there is the hierarchical paradigm of the church, which drew on the monarchial mind-set of the Greco-Roman and medieval worlds. "It is the priest who 'represents' Christ to the people. He is Christ in person; the congregation is the recipient of the church's gifts of grace."[6] Moltmann notes that in Vatican II the Roman Catholic Church adjusted this hierarchical view by including in it the image of the people of God, but still maintained the traditional understanding of tasks and functions.

This paradigm, although still influential in the thinking and practice of the church, gave way following the Reformation to what Moltmann calls the Christological paradigm. "Fellowship with Christ makes the church a brotherly and sisterly community of equals. . . . All are God's children through faith in Christ. All are priest and kings equally. And so the general (better: shared) priesthood of all believers dissolves the division between priest and laity." That at least is the theory, but as Moltmann notes, "practically speaking the distinction between trained theologians and people without any theological training has taken the place of the priestly hierarchy."[7]

The Christological paradigm is now giving way to what Moltmann calls the Charismatic paradigm, in which the gifts of the Spirit are recognized in everyone and are used to build up the body. "No one has a higher or lower position than anyone else with what he or she can contribute to the community."[8]

In describing the functioning of these three paradigms Moltmann explains:

> The hierarchical church distinguished between priest and laity. The Christocentric church made all free and equal as brothers and sisters. But in the charismatic congregations which are growing up, everyone is taken seriously as an expert. Everyone is an expert in his or her own life and personal calling, and all are experts in their original gifts and powers on behalf of the community and its mission.[9]

In true trinitarian fashion, Moltmann maintains that no one of these captures the entire truth about the church. All are needed. All three paradigms act in coequal relationship. However, in the world that is emerging the charismatic paradigm offers a new perspective from which to consider the form and purpose of the church. It also leads us to ask, "What is our congregation's shared ministry?"

## SOME POSSIBLE IMPLICATIONS

Once again, it is important to stress that it is impossible to say what the result of asking this new question might be in any congregation. That depends on the congregation. It is possible, however, to note some possible implications that might follow.

*The importance of roles may decrease and the importance of gifts may increase.* In the past, the structure of most congregations provided for set roles with defined responsibilities. The pastor attended to certain things. The various boards of the church worked in clearly defined areas. The mark of a smooth-running organization was everyone staying within defined areas of responsibilities and fulfilling those responsibilities. The assumption was that this arrangement was permanent and could be followed regardless of the people who were in the roles.

In many ways this definition of roles and responsibilities made sense. What it failed to recognize, however, was the nature of gifts. Not everyone has all the gifts. People don't usually have the same combination of gifts. If people happened to be in a role that included responsibilities for which they were not gifted, the church suffered. Quite often those people were the objects of criticism for not doing what they were supposed to do. And quite often the person who was the object of that criticism was the pastor. He was not a good administrator. She was not a good preacher. He didn't visit the homebound as he should. She didn't relate to the youth very well. Given the nature of spiritual gifts the look-at-all-the-gifts-that-person-doesn't-have game can always be won by those who choose to play it, because no one has them all!

A focus on shared ministry changes all that. It recognizes that the ministry of the church is shared among people who are involved in those ministries for which they are gifted. If the pastor is a great preacher, but not comfortable visiting the homebound, then others in the community assume those responsibilities. Once a congregation claims its shared ministry, it no longer associates predetermined responsibilities with specific roles. Responsibilities are determined and shared among the people as the congregation discovers each person's gifts, including the gifts of the pastor, and people assume those responsibilities for which they are gifted.

*Ministry teams may play a more significant role in the life of the congregation.* In order to take advantage of the variety of gifts that God has bestowed on the congregation to do the work of ministry, people with different gifts will come together to plan and implement the ministry to which they share a common commitment. These teams will be ones that practice what Jeff Woods refers to in his book *Congregational Megatrends* as primary rather than secondary planning.[10] In the traditional church structure, plans are often made by one of the designated boards. Then others are recruited to implement those plans. The board of Christian Education makes the plans for vacation Bible school and then recruits teachers, for example. In primary planning, those who implement also do the planning. They are chosen because they care about the concern that is being addressed. "The only way to ensure that an event will meet people's needs is to involve in the planning process the very people you hope to reach."[11] Primary planning creates a greater sense of ownership and helps to ensure that people are involved in those ministries in which they have interest and for which they have gifts.

*The pastor may let go of traditional ministerial roles.* Shared ministry will only happen if the pastor lets go of traditional ministry roles and the congregation is willing to let him or her do so. There are two dimensions to this issue. It is not easy to let go of those things that have shaped your identity or defined your role in a community. In all honesty, not everyone who serves as a pastor is able to do that. It can be difficult to share the planning of worship with a team when the results are something other than you like or would do on your own. It can challenge your sense of yourself as a pastoral caregiver if others know more about the pastoral needs of members of the community than you do. But this will happen if ministry is truly shared. It takes a strong pastor to not stand in the way. Likewise, members of the congregation will need to be willing to let people other than the pastor take on responsibilities that have traditionally been seen as the role of clergy. I've heard more than one story of a parishioner who complained that no one ever visited her in the hospital when she received regular visits from the pastoral care team, but not from the pastor.

Changing traditional roles and responsibilities in a congregation creates uncertainty, insecurity, and sometimes even a bit of chaos. It can also lead to a new way of seeing and a new way of being. That is what can happen when you start to ask new questions.

# 6

# PLANNED/DISCERNED

*Old Question: "What's our vision and how do we implement it?"*
*New Question: "What's God up to and how do we get on board?"*

In the relatively stable world of modern Christendom everything must have been easier. It was pretty clear what it took for a congregation to do the right thing. It was all about conducting eleven o'clock worship, organizing Sunday school, maintaining a board and committee structure, carrying out long-range and strategic plans, and developing and implementing mission programs or supporting denominational mission efforts. As long as whatever a congregation did contained appropriate amounts of worship (*leitourgia*), education (*kerygma*), fellowship (*koinonia*), and service (*diakonia*) it was fulfilling the fundamental purposes of the church. As long as the Word was rightly preached and the sacraments properly administer a parish could pretty safely assume it was doing God's work. Members of a congregation could plan on the basis of established patterns—quite certain that if they had it right before (which they assumed they did), they could do the same thing and it would still be right.

In a time of rapid and radical change all bets are off on that one. Doing what has always been done before simply isn't going to work. That is one of the reasons there has been a significant focus on vision in recent years. If continuing to do what we have usually done no longer works, we need to develop some sense of what we are now going to be about. So helping a congregation articulate its vision has become one of the "must-have" skills of the pastor. In many cases congregations, following the counsel of pastors, denominational leaders, and consultants, have adopted a secular planning model. In doing so they have usually added a few reminders that some elements of the process need to be a bit different. So, there is the reminder that for the church, prayer is always important and the vision is always God's, but the essence of the model remains the same. All too often the secular model is what really determines the process. The prayers are perfunctory and little effort is made to decide if the vision is truly God's or just the product of the hopes, dreams, and wishes of the people doing the planning. Those hopes, dreams, and wishes may be good ones, but in the church we are about something a bit different.

"What's our vision and how do we implement it?" is not a question that will help us faithfully move into the new world that is emerging. Too often our own vision is restricted to those things with which we are familiar. Too often, even if we know we shouldn't, we fall back into old patterns that give preference to the way things are over the way God would like them to be. Too often we orient ourselves toward the institution rather than the world. To increase the possibility that we will overcome these rip currents in our thinking, we need to move back to a more basic question: "What is God up to?" We look for the answer to that question not in what was done before, not in our hopes and dreams, not in the church—but in what is happening in the world right now, for it is the world that God loves and where God is at work. Therefore the new formative question for determining what a church is about is: "What's God up to and how do we get on board?"

The place to begin when dealing with this new question is to admit that it is an exceedingly difficult one to answer. History is full of examples of people who believed they knew precisely what God was up to and whom we, with the benefit of hindsight, know were clearly mistaken. More immediately, most of us have encountered people who have gone through all the right spiritual practices to determine God's will, only to reach a decision that was later proven to be decidedly off base. The truth is most people and most congregations are not very practiced at sorting through the myriad possibilities that exist to determine what God is about in their particular neck of the woods. But unless a church begins there, there is little hope of being about God's work.

Another of the reasons why answering the "What's God up to?" question is so difficult is there is an array of deeply held, conflicting opinions about what God is like and what God is doing in the world. There are a considerable number of people in the church today who are convinced that if Jesus had come as a twenty-first-century American instead of a first-century Jew, he would listen to NPR, vote a straight Democratic ticket, proudly proclaim himself to be a religious progressive, condemn virtually all the recent decisions of the Supreme Court, and follow Rachel Maddow on Twitter. And, of course, there are also those who believe he would be a devotee of Fox News and a member of the NRA, believe in trickle-down economics, oppose immigration reform, vote for every Tea Party candidate, and fervently support armed intervention in any situation that was perceived to threaten the security of the United States.

The fact that good people who consider themselves Christians and have a meaningful personal relationship with Jesus Christ have such diametrically opposite opinions should alert us to the fact that something deeper is going on in all of this. We could, of course, simply assume that those who disagree with us are delusional, under the influence of the devil, victims of a deprived childhood, caught up in their own sinful selfishness, naïve do-gooders whose sheltered lives make them oblivious to the way the world really works, or just plain ignorant. In selecting any one of these options we might be considered at least mildly delusional ourselves, however. If we consider these radically different opinions about Jesus thoughtfully, my guess is that the first thing they tell us is that neither position is correct. A twenty-first-century American Jesus would most likely confound, confuse, and probably anger most, if not all, of us. He simply wouldn't fit into whatever boxes we built for him any more than he would fit into the box Peter wanted to build for him at the Transfiguration.

The second thing these divergent opinions might tell us is that however we approach this issue of what it means to follow Jesus in twenty-first-century America, we had best do so with a great deal of humility. That doesn't mean that we cannot be passionate about what we believe are the places and issues we, as followers of Jesus, should be involved in, but rather that a humble passion that accepts the reality we could be wrong, that we could have misread Jesus completely, is appropriate. It also doesn't mean that some people aren't more right than wrong on important issues and other people aren't more wrong than right. There is, after all, right and wrong in the world and on basic issues of love and justice we all need to make decisions about where we stand and what we will do. Remembering that Jesus doesn't fit our boxes and maintaining some measure of humility, however, can help us negotiate the complex terrain of discerning what God is up to in the world and deciding how we will join in.

As is usually the case, the Bible is an important resource for us when we're thinking about God and what God might be about. Personally, I like the way Ephesians handles it. Today's English Version puts it this way:

> In all his wisdom and insight God did what he had purposed, and made known to us the secret plan he had already decided to complete by means of Christ. This plan, which God will complete when the time is right, is to bring all creation together, everything in heaven and on earth, with Christ as head. (Ephesians 1:8b–10, TEV)

God's plan, the thing that God is up to, is "to bring all creation together, everything in heaven and on earth, with Christ as head." In other words, God is about the redemption of all creation, getting all creation in right relationship with itself and with God. That's what happens when Christ is head. The implications of this are overwhelming! They touch virtually every aspect of our being—encompassing what happens at work, in the community, at home; embracing business and government—including us, the birds of the air and the fish of the sea, all creation. This is what God is about. This is why Christ came, lived, died, and rose from the dead. It's about a whole lot more than salvation for humans or providing a means of going to heaven when we die. It is about the redemption of all creation.

Colossians makes this same point, putting it in the past tense, as something already accomplished through Christ:

> For it was by God's own decision that the Son has in himself the full nature of God. Through the Son, then, God decided to bring the whole universe back to himself. God made peace through his Son's blood on the cross and so brought back to himself all things, both on earth and in heaven. (Colossians 1:19–20)

And Romans reminds us that this is what God is about as Paul speaks of waiting for the final coming of Christ:

> All of creation waits with eager longing for God to reveal his children. For creation was condemned to lose its purpose, not of its own will, but because God willed it to be so. Yet there was the hope that creation itself would one day be set free from its slavery to decay and would share the glorious freedom of the children of God. For we know that up to the present time all of creation groans with pain, like the pain of childbirth. (Romans 8:19–22)

God is concerned for all creation and its redemption, not just us and our salvation. But we have a role to play in this great work of God. Ephesians points the way:

> It is by God's grace that you have been saved. In our union with Christ Jesus he raised us up with him to rule with him in the heavenly world. He did this to demonstrate for all time to come the extraordinary greatness of his grace in the love he showed us in Christ Jesus. For it is by God's grace that you have been saved through faith. It is not the result of your own efforts, but God's gift, so that no one can boast about it. God has made us what we are, and in our union with Christ Jesus he has created us for a life of good deeds, which he has already prepared for us to do. (Ephesians 2:5b–10, TEV)

Each one of us was created by God for a purpose. Each one of us was saved for a purpose—to join God's work in the redemption of all creation. These are the good deeds that have been prepared for us to do!

What God is up to concerns all things, seeking to bring all creation into right relationship. It is to the world, not the church, then, that we should look in our search for the work that God is about—which is why we ask, "How do we send them out?" rather than "How do we bring them in?" And it is those who are involved in the world who can best provide insight into the way we can best become a part of this thing that God is up to—which is why we ask, "What is our congregation's shared ministry?" not "What should the pastor do?"

Acknowledging the difficulty of the task, we can best approach the question through a process of discernment. Actually, discernment is important in answering all the new questions, but considering discernment now as we focus on what God is up to and how we can join in seems particularly appropriate. We will look at the process in this chapter, knowing that what is said here can be used elsewhere as well.

I use the word "discernment" cautiously and somewhat reluctantly, because it has in many ways become a buzzword that allows those of us in churches to add a veneer of piety to what is in reality just a typical decision-making or problem-solving process. I think, for example, of the agenda for a meeting of a religious organization I once saw that indicated each of the items the group would discuss and decide about. At the end of each work session, fifteen minutes was allotted to "discernment." I'm not certain what type of discerning the meeting planners anticipated in that time, but we can safely assume that I am talking about something else.

Discernment as we will explore it here is, in the words of Danny Morris and Charles M. Olsen in *Discerning God's Will Together*, "to see to the heart of the matter with spiritual eyes; from God's vantage point, to see beneath the surface of events, through illusions within human systems, and beyond the immediate and the transient."[1] Suzanne Farnham, Stephanie Hull, and Taylor McLean in *Grounded in God: Listening Hearts Discernment for Group Deliberations* describe it as a means of "distinguishing the voice of God from other voices that speak to us, . . . a prayerful, informed, and intentional attempt to sort through these voices to get in touch with God's Spirit at work in a situation and to develop a sense of the direction in which the Spirit is leading."[2] Pierre Wolff, who uses Ignatian spiritually as the basis for discernment, describes it as "a systematic process of working in time with our intellect and affective self (emotions), according to a value system illumined by faith."[3]

Discernment cannot be reduced to a process that one follows step by step. There are, however, a number of disciplines that are essential to discernment.[4] All of these disciplines are done in conversation not only with others, but with God in prayer. That's why I have not included a separate discipline of prayer. It is a central and essential part of each of the disciplines.

*Slow down.* We live in a frenzied and frantic world of instant gratification. If there is a problem, it needs to be solved—sooner rather than later. If there is a conflict, it needs to be resolved—sooner rather than later. If someone is unhappy, they need to be placated—sooner rather than later. There is an almost compulsive rush to decision and solution whenever we are confronted with something that is not the way we or someone whose opinions we need to honor wants it to be. And in most cases people look to the leader to take care of whatever presents itself as the problem.

An essential discipline of discernment is to slow down, to change the pace of our deciding. Slowing down accomplishes several purposes. First, it allows us to become more familiar with the situation, to live with and begin to understand it better. Second, it increases the chances of something other than a firsthand, off-the-cuff, flying-by-the-seat-of-our-pants solution. Third, it creates space and space is essential if the Holy Spirit is to be a part of what we are about. Morris and Olsen explain, "In discernment, we assume the presence and active involvement of the Holy Spirit. People hoping to discern the yearnings of God will be sensitive to the presence, the initiatives, and the movement of the Spirit because without the Holy Spirit's involvement there can be no spiritual discernment."[5]

*Focus.* For discernment to be helpful there needs to be a clear and common understanding of the concern. Most often this will come in the form of a question. So, getting the question right is essential. This may be more difficult and take more time than expected. Sharing the perceptions of the situation by those involved and reaching a genuine consensus on what the group is seeking to discern as it works together is essential.

*Let go.* Most of us, when confronted with an issue that concerns us, have a previously formed perspective, perhaps even a solution. Additionally, an array of other factors from feelings to memories to ego is usually present. To be open to the work of the group and the Holy Spirit, we need to let go of all of these in order to be truly open to God's leading. This isn't easy. It might mean giving up things we cherish. It also means committing one's self to doing God's will even before knowing what that will is.

*Listen.* When we let go of our assumptions, we can enter into dialogue rather than discussion. Drawing on the work of David Bohm, Peter Senge makes this discussion-dialogue distinction in *The Fifth Discipline*. He notes that when we suspend our assumptions about an issue, we open ourselves more fully to what others are saying, which in turn opens us to seeing things we haven't seen before.[6] Suspending assumptions also releases us from the practice of using the time in which others are speaking to decide what we will say next, so that we can truly listen to what others are saying. This listening is about more than words. It involves feelings, body language, facial expressions—all those ways through which we communicate with each other.

*Connect.* Exploring possible connections between thoughts, statements, and issues is important. How does one idea relate to another? Do even opposing ideas hold something in common? How might one idea build upon another? Connecting extends beyond ideas shared in the group, however. It also includes connecting to the biblical story and to other traditions of the faith and of the congregation. Is there a story in the Bible that might provide insight? Is there a practice of the church that would help us with this?

*Probe.* This is the discipline of exploring consequences and implications, considering the values inherent in an option, reflecting on ways the option might lead to unexpected consequences. Rational analysis is important here, but more is involved. The authors of *Grounded in God* make this point: "Sound rational analysis based on the best available information is crucial to good discernment. Yet spiritual discernment goes beyond the analytical to engage our senses, feelings, imaginations, and intuition as we wrestle with issues. It often points to a decision, but it is **not** problem-solving."[7]

*Wait.* Waiting is essential. Sometimes the answers don't come. Sometimes consensus eludes us. Even when a group is on the cusp of something that seems right, it may be important to stop and wait, to let things rest for a bit, to listen more deeply to what the heart and the Spirit might be trying to say.

*Settle.* There comes a time to settle on a direction. It may take awhile to get to this point—sometimes days or months. But settling isn't about chronological time; it's about *kairos*, God's time. *Grounded in God* contains a helpful list of qualities that are likely to be present when a right consensus has been reached and it is time to settle: peace (a sense of rightness), joy that leads to energy for action, a persistence with which an idea keeps coming, a convergence of ideas and opinions, fruitfulness (producing meaningful results). They may not all be present every time, but the presence of several is a strong indication of the group being attuned to God's will.[8] Sometimes a deliberate process of seeking consensus is needed. Votes are not taken, but each person is given the opportunity to state his or her thoughts, ensuring that no one wishes to block the action that is being proposed.

*Rest.* Often it is wise not to act immediately, but to wait yet again. This waiting allows everyone to sense how things seem the next day or the next week, to listen again to the heart and the Spirit. This, too, is part of the slowing down that is essential to discernment.

The precise way in which these disciplines can most effectively impact a congregation depends upon a variety of factors. These include people's level of comfort with discernment, the amount of time that is available for a decision to be made, and the willingness of the congregation to entrust a group with the power to decide. Some congregations like to know where they are headed. In that context, describing the full discernment process at the beginning would be helpful, provided it's clear

that there is always a movement back and forth among the various disciplines that are involved. Other congregations are more comfortable with
loosely structured conversation. In that context it might be best to take
a "stealth" approach to discernment. In this case, the overall process
might not be discussed, but the leadership would guide the group as it
develops the disciplines in its life together, while at the same time presenting possibilities for action to see if discussion of them will lead to a
consensus.

## SOME POSSIBLE IMPLICATIONS

*Letting go of the congregation's focus on its own concerns may be essen-
tial.* Many congregations, especially those that are struggling, develop an
inward focus. They are concerned about financial viability, maintaining
programs, filling offices and boards. This is quite natural, but it is also
deadly. Refocusing the congregation on what God is up to in the world is
difficult, but essential. Simply asking the question may create resistance.
Both practically and theologically this shift is needed, however. Chances
of survival are greater if a church has a strong mission emphasis. Whether
it survives in the long run or not, a mission emphasis aligns a congregation more fully with the work of the reign of God.

 *A new understanding of stewardship and tithing may be needed.* Stewardship has become a growing concern for many church leaders and
congregations in recent years. Part of the reason for that is an increased
awareness of our responsibility for all of God's creation and the importance of being good stewards of that creation. In all honesty, however,
another reason is that congregations and denominations need to generate
more income. A renewed focus on stewardship, leaders hope, will increase giving, especially from those who have not had a sense of institutional loyalty instilled in them from birth. Additionally, tithing has received more emphasis as a spiritual discipline in some congregations,
both because it is a genuine and helpful discipline that can enhance spiritual growth, but also because it has potential to increase giving to the
church.

When the formative question becomes "What is God up to and how do we get on board?" the congregation and denomination may not receive as much funding, because people will be supporting other places they see God at work. In the past, a discussion about tithing usually assumed that this portion of one's income would be directed, if not exclusively at least primarily, to the church. If, however, the primary criteria in giving is to support any of those places where God is at work in the world, the amount given directly to the church may change. The reduced funding to which this leads will not be easy for congregations and denominations already struggling financially to handle, but less money for the church is a possible implication of this change in the formative question we ask.

*Some people may believe that discernment conflicts with democratic principles.* Congregations in the United States, especially those in the free-church tradition, are in most cases committed to the democratic principle. When there is an issue to be decided, everyone gets a say and then a vote is taken. Whatever side gets more votes prevails. The time spent in this process of deciding is usually brief. The rules that are followed (thanks to General Roberts) are, if convoluted, at least written down, so they can be followed. A decision gets made and you move on. The discernment process is radically different. There are no motions, just questions. There are no rules, just disciplines. There are no votes, just a search for consensus. Those who are steeped in Roberts' Rules of Order will most likely find this a difficult, time-consuming process that offers no clear way to make a decision. Be warned! It may work best to move gradually from Roberts-based decision making to discernment, bringing elements of discernment into a more traditional democratic process. Other churches may find that simply taking time to explain the process and why it is important will overcome resistance.

*Patience may be required because of the amount of time discernment most often takes.* Everyone involved, especially the leaders, will need patience. It will, as the above paragraph indicates, take time for people to become comfortable with this new way of making decisions. Discernment itself takes time. It is impossible to schedule a decision as you can a vote. There is often a necessary waiting game until a real consensus develops. All of this requires patience.

*A deeper and broader sense of commitment to the mission of the church may develop.* In discernment there are no winners and losers. The process itself enables significant sharing of information and leads to broad-based agreement. All of this enhances the level of commitment people will have for those things in which the church is involved. Because there is an explicit spiritual dimension to a discernment process, decisions made through that process may be seen in a faith perspective. It is no longer just "we decided to do this," but rather "we discerned that this is what God wants us to be about." That alone makes a world of difference.

In asking, "What is God up to and how do we get on board?" a congregation determines what it will do in a new way. This way has the potential to bring God's work in the world to the forefront, reducing its focus on internal issues. The concern is no longer whether the congregation will be around for centuries or just a few more years. What matters is that for as long as possible and in every way possible, the people of the congregation are doing the work of God.

# 7

# SURVIVE/SERVE

*Old Question: "How do we survive?" (Or in churches that are less desperate, "How do we structure?")*
*New Question: "How do we serve?"*

There is hardly a congregation around today that hasn't struggled with the question of how to fill all the positions the bylaws establish. Sometimes there simply aren't enough members to fill all the positions. But even in congregations that have enough people, those people are often not willing to serve. Hectic lifestyles, multiple and conflicting priorities, the noninstitutional orientation of postmodernity all conspire against a structure that worked for decades.

Many congregations have moved beyond the structure question to the survival question. It's no longer just about people; it's about money. The demands of building maintenance and staff salaries have gone beyond the resources of the congregation. Funding to support ministry and mission, which might already have been cut to the bare bones, is often being eliminated completely in an effort to balance the budget. The lack of both people and money is viewed as an internal issue, so (if denominational polity permits) bylaws are rewritten to reduce the number of positions and shorten the length of terms, fundraisers are instituted, grants are solicited, giving is encouraged. When none of these strategies produce the desired results, the congregation rediscovers the Bible concept of stewardship and hopes it will increase the giving of those who are there. Often the congregation will also launch some type of church-growth effort whose major motivation is to increase the number of people and the amount of money available to support the structure and the budget. The underlying assumption is that a larger congregation will provide the resources needed.

All these strategies make sense—until the congregation discovers, usually after a significant amount of effort, that the situation hasn't really gotten any better and in many cases has deteriorated even further.

Congregations find themselves in this predicament because structure and survival issues are typically symptoms of another concern. At its core the issue is not about people and money. It is really about identity and purpose. The fundamental question that needs to be answered is not about structure or survival, but about purpose. That, as we noted in the previous chapter, is directly related to what God is up to in the world. Congregations, as we noted in chapter 4, do not exist for themselves. They exist to further the reign of God in the world. An internal focus is inevitably a dead-end street for churches—a virtual rearranging of the deck chairs on the Titanic—because it is a denial of the very reason churches exist, a rejection of the commission they were given by Christ.

One way to enter into the outward focus that is needed for congregations is to ask, "How do we serve?" In asking this question, congregations can begin to align themselves more fully with a gospel that asks that we deny ourselves (Mark 8:34) and reminds us that to save our lives we need to lose our lives (Mark 8:35). This new question helps the congregation move its focus from itself and its needs to others and their needs. This is the essence of the agape love of which the gospel speaks. As Pierre Wolff in his book on discernment notes: "Agape means loving, but loving as doing and working for the good and growth of others. . . . It may or may not include a warm feeling of empathy. Above all, it is service."[1] In asking this question congregations can reorient themselves to their more basic purpose.

Remember, dealing with this new question (or any of the new questions I am offering) won't necessarily bring new people and money to your congregation or ensure its survival. It may, but there is no guarantee. What it will do is change perceptions of what the real needs are, which will in turn put the need for people and money in a new perspective. What it will do is encourage the congregation to focus its energy in a way that demonstrates the real reason it exists.

Reorienting a congregation away from surviving and structuring to serving is a significant challenge. A congregation will need to set different priorities, to refocus its concern, and let go of what seem to be compelling and urgent needs. Each of these changes requires learning, which means that it is an example of the adaptive challenge that we described in chapter 3. Because it is an adaptive challenge, the writings of Ronald Heifetz and Marty Linsky offer us some important insights for making the transition from the old survival question to the new serving question.

Before we take a look at those insights, however, let's take a brief excursion to explore the impact that anxiety about survival has on an organization and why this makes this particular transition a difficult one to manage.

Concerns about survival create anxiety. Change also creates anxiety. All systems, including congregations, seek homeostasis and become anxious whenever the status quo is disrupted. When anxiety is present, people in the congregation will most likely begin to exhibit a variety of reactive behaviors, such as denial, blaming, and overboard enthusiasm. These are usually attempts to maintain stability, but they more often serve to increase the number of challenges the system will need to face.

You can blame these unhelpful behaviors on our brains and the way they work. The amygdala, the most primitive part of the brain, is all about survival. As such it is reactive; that is, it reacts to threats without thinking. This can be a good thing, because it allows us to respond quickly to dangerous situations. But reactive responses are not the best way to deal with every situation in which we find ourselves. In the past reactive responses were seen as attempts to flee, to fight, or to freeze. Recent research indicates that women are more likely to have a "tend and befriend" response. The common feature in all of these responses is that they are automatic reactions to a situation that is deemed to be threatening. That's how the amygdala works.

Thankfully, we don't usually function out of our amygdalas. The cortex or thinking part of the brain has the ability to rein in the amygdala, so our actions are less reactive, more reasoned. This part of the brain develops later than other parts and is not functioning at full capacity until the mid-twenties. But even for adults, in situations of significant stress there is a short-circuit in the brain that prevents the cortex from exercising its thinking function. Furthermore, the amygdala can not only short-circuit the cortex, it can highjack it. When it does, the thinking function of the cortex works with the amygdala and develops seemingly rational explanations for irrational behavior. In a time of rapid and radical change anxiety is already great. Concern about survival of an institution you love increases that anxiety even further. In a situation such as this, the short-circuiting and highjacking of the thinking brain by the amygdala are likely to happen more frequently. When they do, the ability to think creatively about options is diminished, either/or thinking becomes more predominant, and the degree of fatalism increases. In a time when creative hope is essential, it is even less likely to appear.

The difficulty of dealing with these reactive responses is one of the reasons I believe that every church leadership team should include someone who enjoys teaching middle-school students. I first came upon this notion by observing middle-school teachers deal with situations in the church much more effectively than I seemed able to do. There was something about the way they were able to respond to what appeared to me to be irrational behavior that left me in awe. They could handle situations better because they had learned to deal with student behavior—behavior that we can now explain scientifically. Because the cortex develops later than other parts of the brain, middle-school students quite naturally operate with an amygdala bias. That is, they are more reactive, less able to control their actions by thinking about what to do. In order to enjoy teaching middle-school students, therefore, you need to be able to deal with this dynamic. And if you can deal with it in them, you can also deal with it in adults who become reactive when their anxiety is heightened.

Taking a clue from the middle-school teachers I've watched, I've seen that the key to dealing with all of this is not to become reactive yourself. It's easy to get hooked by the reactive behavior of others so that you react rather than respond to their behavior. You need a highly functioning cortex in order to maintain your cool. It is one of the key requirements for being that nonanxious presence we talked about in chapter 1.

Being a nonanxious presence doesn't mean, of course, we should be working to keep everyone happy and less anxious. Stress and anxiety are necessary components of change. Without them, and often without a healthy dose of them, change is impossible. The thinking brain understands the need for anxiety. Simply working to lessen anxiety could very well be a reactive response based in our own need to avoid anxiety! As Peter Steinke reminds us, "Real leaders ask hard questions and knock people out of their comfort zones. Then they manage the resulting distress."[2] That, in a nutshell, is also one of the insights that Ronald Heifetz offers.

The notion of the adaptive challenge has become commonplace in organizations today. There is simply no doubt that organizations, including congregations, need to meet any number of adaptive challenges. Meeting the challenge requires learning by those involved, because no one yet knows the solution. The process leading to that solution always involves a conflict of values. Learning is hard work. Conflict is unpleasant. So, meeting an adaptive challenge, as necessary as it may be, is a challenge in itself! It is, in fact, an impossible challenge for many organizations and congregations, and one of the primary reasons they may not survive in this time when deep change is essential.

Thankfully, Heifetz not only presents the concept of the adaptive challenge, he also provides some significant insight into the strategies we can use to meet it. There are a multitude of resources that describe his insights. *Leadership on the Line*, the book he coauthored with Marty Linsky, provides the best look at strategies for meeting adaptive challenges. A few of those strategies have particular importance for us as we seek to move from a focus on surviving to one on serving.

*Keep the big picture in mind.* It is essential to maintain a sense of the big picture through what Heifetz calls "getting on the balcony." This is about stepping back regularly to observe the interactions that are taking place, including your own, to see points of resistance and support, to assess the level of stress. For our purposes stepping back also enables us to observe how well people understand the need to change the formative questions in general and the specific new questions in particular. Are there signs, for example, of a movement from survival to serving in people's conversations, in the decisions they are making, the actions they are taking?

*Involve the people in finding the answer.* Giving the problem back to the people, another of Heifetz's strategies, is essential because the solution to an adaptive challenge needs to come from those involved. It also sounds a cautionary note about the urge leaders experience to provide answers, to be the expert, to present the solution. That is often what members of congregations expect from their leaders, but to do that as you deal with this or any of the questions would be a surefire way to ensure that real change—change that requires new learning—won't happen because the congregation as a whole will not experience the need for change and develop an understanding and commitment to that change. The best strategy for involving people may be to do nothing more than ask, "What would happened if we set aside our focus on survival for a bit and began to ask ourselves how can we best serve those in our community who need us?" It may be that this is enough. If it isn't, then try asking this question again. Telling stories about the way the church has served the community in the past and stories from the Bible about serving may also help them to move beyond a focus on survival. You might even suggest some ways in which the congregation could begin to serve others in the community. But don't give them the answer! Don't do it, because you don't know it. They are the only ones who can decide what a focus on serving rather than surviving might mean for them. If you falter and take the lead in developing a new focus on serving, I can almost guarantee that it will be among the first things to go after you do.

*Keep the stress at a manageable level.* Any organization can handle only so much stress. Some is essential, because without it, people will see no reason to change. Too much is counterproductive because it overwhelms and demoralizes. Heifetz's insight regarding stress is to control the temperature. That is, do what can be done to manage the level of stress. You can ask only so many questions, make so many suggestions without increasing the annoyance factor to an unproductive level. You can only encourage engagement with a limited number of new ideas without overwhelming people. When reactivity reaches a certain point it is essential to tone things down a bit, to stop the questions, to focus on the familiar and things the congregation enjoys and can accomplish. That's one way to reduce the stress. It's important to set a limit on this, however, because some level of stress is essential in order for the congregation to be willing to change. After people have caught their collective breath, you can begin to ask the questions again, recognizing that doing so may make people uncomfortable but this is necessary in order to move from a survival to serving mentality. Of course, one of the important dimensions of this process is monitoring your own level of stress and your comfort with it. More than one leader has moved into stress-reduction mode not because the others couldn't handle it, but because he or she couldn't. Know thyself!

If anything I've said seems to imply that making this transition from a survival mentality to a serving mentality is not exceedingly difficult, I want to correct that misconception. It is hard, really hard to lead a congregation through this change. When any person or group is fighting for its life, they find it all but impossible to think of anyone but themselves. It is easy to develop any number of rationales for tending to the congregation's own needs before reaching out to serve others. This approach may be true for airplane oxygen masks, but it is not true for the church. The church exists to serve. Its purpose, as we will explore in the next chapter, is to make the reign of God more fully present in its time and place. When it forgets this it becomes a church in name only. It loses its reason for being. The driving, energizing force of the Holy Spirit is no longer present. The very survival it seeks becomes impossible.

# SOME POSSIBLE IMPLICATIONS

*Those who refuse to let go of an inward focus may be a gift.* Even though all the reasons, both theological and practical, for moving from a survival to a serving mentality are presented and discussed over and over, some people will not be able to move beyond asking, "How do we survive?" It is best to see this stance as a potential asset. Some people do need to be concerned about the physical and fiscal issues of the congregation. Those who continue to be focused on survival can play that role. Those who do make the shift to the serving mentality can move the congregation into new ways of being, always honoring the ones who keep things together on the home front.

*The congregation may be surprised at its ability to serve.* If some in the congregation are able to move beyond a survival mentality, look to those in the community that are in need, and begin to serve them, they may be surprised by what they can accomplish. Often a reluctance to serve is based in an assumption that a struggling church does not have the resources to help others. This is especially true for smaller churches. David Ray, a small-church pastor and consultant, reminds us: "Smaller churches concerned more about survival than service sometimes forget that making a difference is the path from survival to life. . . . There are little churches everywhere that that are making things better, helping out in real ways, loving their neighbors, making their communities more livable, and reaching around the world."[3] Even little acts of kindness and hospitality can lead a congregation to serve others in significant ways.

*Your own amygdala may do you in.* As you are involved in the process of changing questions, it is important to keep tabs on your own level of stress and reactivity. That may be especially true as you deal with this new question, because the need to move the congregation's focus from surviving to serving seems self-evident. It is basic to an understanding of the church and its purpose. It seems obvious that a church should be more concerned about serving others than surviving. Just because this understanding of the church's purpose makes sense, however, doesn't mean that everyone can agree. Of all the questions, this one probably has the greatest potential to touch some very tender nerves among parishioners.

Longtime members have a significant emotional attachment to the church and its building, which lies at the heart of their concern for survival. If you are working to move the congregation from a survival to a serving mentality, the emotional commitment that some members have to the congregation as it has been in the past can lead to a significant degree of frustration for you. You may become highly frustrated by their inability to understand a need that seems so evident to you. If frustration reaches that high level, reactivity is just around the corner, so watch your amygdala and take the steps you need to take to reengage your thinking brain!

German theologian Jürgen Moltmann reminds us: "The church cannot understand itself alone. It can only truly comprehend its mission and its meaning, its roles and its functions in relation to others." One of those essential relationships is "to the historical situation in the world, the situation in which it is set and which it takes into account in attempting to interpret 'the signs of the times.'"[4] That relationship is with those outside the church, for they are the ones who help shape its mission to the world. In serving them we make clear to others, and more importantly ourselves, what the church's true purpose is.

# 8

# SAVE/SIGN

*Old Question: "What are we doing to save people?"*
*New Question: "What are we doing to make the reign of God more present in this time and place?"*

Old-time evangelism was about saving people. In its most basic form it was about getting them to accept Jesus Christ as their Lord and Savior, so they would go to heaven when they died. One popular evangelism visitation program asked the question, "If you were to die tonight, do you know for sure that you will be with God in heaven?" To be saved, people confessed their sins and prayed that Jesus come into their heart so their sins could be forgiven. It was the responsibility of the church to save as many people as possible.

This is admittedly a rather extreme example, and many churches and Christians would not be comfortable with, let alone engage in, this approach to evangelism. Some would be traumatized simply by the use of the word "evangelism!" For many churches, the old question would be more along the lines of "What are we doing to help people?" And yet the assumption behind this helping question is in many ways quite similar to that behind the saving question. The essence of the assumption behind both of them is, "We have something that others need and we have a responsibility to share it with them." We have already noted in chapter 4 that this assumption also lies behind the need to bring people into the church. There's no doubt that the question about helping people has spawned an array of efforts that have done great good and benefited countless people. The efforts include everything from medical and agricultural work that has improved the lives of millions to a knitted shawl that brought comfort to one person. The underlying dynamic here, however, is essentially the same as with old-style evangelism. It's about giving others something we already have that we believe will make their lives better.

From a Christian perspective, neither saving nor helping people, although worthy desires, is the ultimate reason the church exists. Biblically, the main thrust of the ministry of Jesus was the announcement of the coming of the reign of God. Saving and helping were certainly a part of that, but only a part. Jesus' ministry of healing was to demonstrate the presence of the reign of God. So, when John's disciples came to Jesus asking if he was the Messiah, he replied by having them look at what was happening in his ministry—all signs of the in-breaking reign of God: "The blind receive their sight, the lame walk, the lepers are cleansed, the deaf hear, the dead are raised, and the poor have good news brought to them" (Matthew 11:5). And in Luke's gospel, Jesus selects a passage from Third Isaiah and reads it in the synagogue in Nazareth, thus proclaiming the reign of God (Luke 4:16–21). The purpose of the church, as we noted in chapter 4, is to serve God's mission by making the reign of God more fully present in the world. It is to be a sign of the reign of God present in this world.

Theologically, as we noted in chapter 6, the big thing God is up to is the redemption of all creation, not just saving or helping individuals. This means that Jesus didn't come, as the Nicene Creed states, "for us and our salvation"—at least not just for that or in the highly personal way that phrase is usually interpreted. Jesus came to announce and initiate the coming of the reign of God and the redemption of creation that would bring. God's reign has come in the teaching, preaching, and ministry of Jesus, but it is not yet fully present. In the words of New Testament scholar N. T. Wright, the reign of God is "a present reality, in which people can share, but which still awaits some sort of final validation."[1]

From both biblical and theological perspectives, the better question for congregations to ask is, "What are we doing to make the reign of God more present in this time and place?" It is about the way in which we do the good deeds God has already prepared for us to do that Ephesians 2 talks about. When the formative question we ask is about the reign of God, we begin to see what we are about from a different perspective. It is no longer primarily a matter of what we have that we can give to others who need it, but rather the way in which participation in God's work offers all of us what we seek for our lives, for others, and for all creation. The emphasis becomes more communal than individual. The focus is the present rather than the future, for it is grounded in history and concerned about what we can do right now. And at the same time the concern is the future rather than the present, for its motivation and hope are that a time will truly come when God's will is done on earth as it is in heaven.

The redemption of all creation is a pretty big undertaking. Obviously, it is not possible for any one congregation, denomination, or even the entire Church to accomplish. God is the only one who can do it. But even the smallest congregation has a role to play. In discerning that role, two dimensions of congregational life are particularly helpful: the gifts of those who are there and the DNA or code of the congregation. Gifts and congregational code both point to the particular way in which individuals and congregations can be engaged in the good deeds that God has already prepared for them to do.

We explored the concept of gifts in chapter 5, noting the way it supports an understanding of shared ministry. Now we look at them as a way to help a congregation discern the particular role it can play in the redemption of all creation. In its simplest form, an understanding of gifts reveals this truth: the role a congregation plays in the redemption of all creation is one for which the people have been given the gifts. If some people in the congregation have the gift of teaching, what might that say about tutoring students in a local school or developing a program in a prison or beginning an effort in English as a second language? If some have the gift of compassion, what about involvement in a hospice or visiting the homebound in the community or developing a food bank? If some have a gift that sensitizes them to issues of justice, what about involvement in efforts to combat racism or poverty or discrimination based on sexual orientation? If some have a gift related to finances, what about a way to help people lessen their debt or secure needed loans or manage their household budget? The key is to discover the gifts that have already been given to those in the congregation and to explore the ways in which those gifts might be used to share God's love more fully with the world.

Quite often the key to discerning gifts is simply to consider what people enjoy doing, what seems to come easily. The next step would be to see if there are others who share that gift and to explore ways in which these gifts can be used in the world, particularly to meet needs that are evident in the community. Here a cautionary note is needed. Most processes that have been developed to help people to discern their gifts have an institutional bias to them. That is, they often lead the person back to that place in the church where the gifts can be used. If the gift is teaching, it is to be used in the Sunday school. If a person's gift is compassion, that person is encouraged to join a visitation team. If someone's gift is related to finances, he or she should become a trustee. While not discounting the importance of any of those roles, here the focus is not in the church, but outside the church, meeting the most pressing needs of the community. That is where the gifts are to be used.

The second concept that can help focus a congregation's involvement in the redemption of all creation is what has been termed congregational DNA or code. The notion here is that there is something in the lifeblood of a congregation, often going back as far as its founding, that provides a sense of identity. A congregation's code can be difficult to discover. In his book *Transforming Church*, Kevin Ford gets at it this way:

> [Churches] have a relationship to a fixed point, which serves as a true north . . . the church's code. Every church has its own unique code that defines its identity and clarifies its focus. Code can be tricky to define. We can talk about code as the essence or soul of a church. We can talk about what code does, which is to shape the face of how the church displays itself to the world. Code shapes tradition, values, and mission.

Code is not usually rational. Most often, it reveals itself indirectly and symbolically, through the myths, heroes, and stories that give a church its texture and flavor.[2]

As a congregation seeks to move out into the world engaging in the work God is about, it is vital that it know its code. Whatever it does needs to resonate with the code; that is, it needs to be an expression of the church's identity. When the work of God in the world and the congregation's code intersect, vibrant, faithful, and effective ministry can happen. If, on the other hand, a congregation acts in a way that is incongruent with its code, it will likely not have either the energy or creativity that it needs for vibrant ministry. All that will be left for the congregation to do is adopt a program the denomination or some other group has prepared or copy what some other church has done.

As Kevin Ford indicates, discovering a congregation's code is in many ways an art. Most often it is not written down or articulated. In many cases it's not even conscious. Instead it is found in the symbols that hold meaning for the people and in the traditions they cherish. Quite often the code goes back to the founding of the church, even if it was decades or even centuries earlier. There was something essential to the founding of the church that has endured through the generations. Ford points to four ways in which code becomes apparent: myths, rituals, heroes, and visuals.

*Myths.* "Myths symbolize the story line and historic meaning of a church. They explain in story form what the church is all about. . . . Typically, a myth tells the story of the founding of the church or key passages in a church's growth and development."[3]

I served as pastor of the First Baptist Church in Plymouth, Massachusetts for a number of years. When it was founded in 1809 it was the first non-Congregational church in town, which meant it was the first church in town that couldn't in some way trace itself back to the Pilgrims. In Plymouth that is a really big deal! One of the Congregational pastors in town is reported to have asked, "What are we to do with these Baptists? They are turning the town upside down!" So part of the church's identity from the beginning, its code, was that it was not among the movers and shakers of the community; its natural orientation was toward those who were marginal and maybe even to turn the town upside down. That "code" still informs how the church sees itself.

*Rituals.* "Rituals symbolize the beliefs, archetypes, behavior patterns, and ideals of a church. They are collective activities that do not serve a pragmatic purpose but that the church considers socially and even spiritually essential."[4]

The church was famous in the town for the three dinners it served annually. New members, old members, former members were mobilized to prepare and serve a dinner to about five hundred people. These were events for the entire community and were in many ways as important as Christmas and Easter for the congregation—so much so that people were left on the active membership list of the church even if they only helped out at the dinners. While there may be any number of ways this approach to church membership could be criticized, the importance of the dinners in the life of the congregation says something basic about the church's code. It is a ritual that indicates the way in which it sees itself in relationship to the community and the importance of that for the congregation.

*Heroes.* "A hero is any personality who possesses highly prized characteristics that symbolize the church. . . . Heroes populate the church's myths and give meaning and emotional power to the unfolding story of a community of people."[5]

Jim was a person church members kept talking about even though he had been dead for five years. He was a quiet man, but still a presence in the life of the congregation. He didn't say much, but when he spoke people listened. They didn't always agree, but they listened. Perhaps what he is most remembered for is his opposition to the Vietnam War. As the war began to take its toll, he began a vigil. He stood in the town square every Wednesday afternoon carrying a sign opposing the war. He was there every week, no matter the weather. Over time others joined him. Some were members of the church, but most were people from the town who shared his view that the war was wrong. Even now he is talked about. Even now those members of the church who stood with him are held in esteem. There is something in the code of the church that speaks to quiet persistence in pursuit of peace.

*Visuals.* "Visual style is the symbolic face a church shows to the world. A church's visual style is reflected in its logos, bulletins, Web sites, choice of paint colors, architecture, design, and the way the parking lot flows."[6]

The church had an architectural review committee. Everything that was done in the building needed to meet appropriate colonial standards. One Easter Sunday morning the congregation arrived to discover that someone had painted a swastika in the front door—certainly not in keeping with the standards set by the committee. But it provided a clash of cultures that raised significant questions about the church's code and the way in which it was lived out. There's no doubt that presenting itself well to the community was basic to the code. But what did "well" really mean, especially in a world with swastikas?

The code of a congregation is itself value neutral. Ford explains, "It is neither good nor bad. It just is. The culture that emerges from a church's code, however, can be positive or negative, a conduit for both good and evil."[7] So, for example, an issue for the church I served in Plymouth continues to be what beliefs and actions will follow from its code. Would being marginal lead to a culture of inferiority and a sense that they could not do anything significant, or would it lead members to connect to and support others in the community who were considered "marginal"? Aligning a congregation's code to the work of God in the world is one way to help ensure that the culture that emerges from the code will be a positive one.

## SOME POSSIBLE IMPLICATIONS

*Those with gifts may also need to develop new skills.* When a congregation uses the concept of gifts to help shape its involvement in God's work in the world, it also takes on the responsibility of equipping the gifted for that work. What are the specific skills the gifted people need to do the good deeds that have been prepared for them to do, and how can the congregation support them in developing those gifts? A commitment to help people develop their skills has significant budget implications for a congregation. Most congregations provide funding for their pastor's continuing education, and many fund training for laity in the roles they play in the church. Few churches, however, provide financial support for laity to develop the skills they need for ministry in the world. A congregation that is focused on the use of gifts to make the reign of God more present in the world will find a way to support the development of the skills laity need in order to do that.

*If a congregation is struggling, it may be out of sync with its code.* A person can never really be someone he or she isn't. A person may expend untold effort putting up a front, playing a role, denying his or her true identity, but ultimately it doesn't work. It might be possible to fool others, but there will always be a sense of something missing, something just not right. The same is true for congregations. A congregation that asks the new question of this chapter may struggle to find a way it can best make the reign of God more present in its community. It may try different approaches, but find that none seems to work. If this happens, then it may be that the attempts it has made are not in line with its code. This incongruence makes it difficult to bring people together to act in a positive and effective way. There may be ongoing strife or an undercurrent of discord, or a lack of energy or sense of community. If any of these are present in a congregation, an exploration of code might provide insight into an incongruence between identity and practice. If this is the case, the incongruence can be overcome by developing a better understanding of the congregation's code and then ministering in ways that are in keeping with that code.

A church that finds a way to align itself with the furthering of the reign of God in the world will discover a passion for ministry that astounds. It will likely be amazed by what it does and where this leads. As with all of the changing questions, this doesn't guarantee new members or increased giving. It may, but that is not what this is all about. What matters here, much more than numbers and even survival, is, in whatever state we find ourselves and for however long that may be, we are about the work of the church because it is related to God's intention for creation for which Jesus lived, died, rose from the dead, and will return. It is always and only this faith that sustains us: Christ has died. Christ is risen. Christ will come again.

# Part 3

# Embracing the Dangerous Work of Change

# PART 3 INTRODUCTION

In the previous section we explored a number of new formative questions that congregations can ask in these days of disruption and dislocation. My hope is that simply by letting go of the questions that have so long shaped our approach to ministry and beginning to ask these new questions, we might minister more faithfully. I also cautioned that there are no guarantees that asking new questions will enhance the vitality, size, or financial stability of your congregation.

What I can guarantee is that asking new questions is dangerous work and if you undertake it, you need to prepare yourself to undertake the dangers as well. It is dangerous because just asking new questions requires change, and change always produces a backlash. It is dangerous because dealing with these questions requires a new understanding of meaningful ministry, and that is difficult to develop. It is dangerous because these questions create a whole new set of standards for the way in which we and others assess the work we have done, and those new standards can leave us wondering if what we have been doing really matters.

The dangers are clear and we will explore them further in chapter 9. Thankfully there is a way for us to live in this dangerous environment. This way has more to do with ourselves than it does with others, with who we are than what we know. And, believe it or not, it also offers us the opportunity to enrich our lives and deepen our faith. We'll be looking at that in chapter 10.

# 9

# THE PREDICAMENT

The full title of Ronald Heifetz and Marty Linsky's book on leadership is *Leadership on the Line: Staying Alive through the Dangers of Leading.*[1] This tells us two things: (1) leadership is dangerous, at least if it's done right, and (2) the danger is life-threatening, if not literally then at the very least mentally, psychologically, and spiritually. That, in short, is the predicament we find ourselves in as we attempt to lead in the church today.

In our discussion of adaptive challenges in chapter 7, we noted that all adaptive change involves a conflict of values. While it may seem on the surface that simply asking different questions shouldn't create significant conflict, there is something at work in this that makes conflict inevitable. Each of the contrasting questions discussed in part 2 is based in different values. The values that underlie the desire to bring people into the church, for example, are radically different from those that underlie a yearning to send people out from the church. So, ceasing to focus on bringing in new members is likely to challenge values that some members of the congregation hold dear; persistence in doing so will likely result in conflict.

Given this likelihood of conflict, it will be helpful for us to have some insight into how it may appear and what we can do about it when it does.

Heifetz and Linsky provide a list of dangers that we are likely to encounter as we attempt to reorient a congregation and begin asking these new questions. As a leader, they say, you almost inevitably create a situation in which attempts will be made to marginalize you, divert you, attack you, and seduce you.[2] When we are marginalized we are removed from the action related to the change we are seeking. Clergy can be marginalized in a congregation that operates on the assumption that the pastor should only be concerned about "spiritual" issues. The laity are to make the decisions about the way the church operates, including the leadership and the budget; the pastor should only be involved in worship, pastoral care, and teaching. There are also times those who do not want you involved in a particular concern will attempt to marginalize you by telling you how important your work in another area is, hoping to keep you on the margins of their area of concern. Others can divert us from primary issues by starting brush fires, those petty conflicts or crises that appear now and then in a congregation. They aren't that important, but take a significant amount of time to resolve. In a similar fashion an array of pastoral care concerns may suddenly develop, keeping us from dealing with a significant issue we have raised (such as a movement to one of the new questions).

If our leadership is seen as a threat to traditions and practices that people value or to their power, they can resort to attack in order to undermine our ability to implement the changes we seek. The attack often comes as questioning our skills or focusing on the gifts we don't have (as if anyone had all the gifts that are needed for leadership in a congregation) or making us the issue rather than the issues we are attempting to address. People seduce us with compliments that often in subtle ways keep us beholden to them. Heifetz and Linksy write, "Seduction, marginalization, diversion and attack all serve a function. They reduce the disequilibrium that would be generated were people to address the issues that are taken off the table. They serve to maintain the familiar, restore order, and protect people from the pains of adaptive work."[3]

Our discussion of the ways in which anxiety undercuts thoughtful action in chapter 7 also points to a potential predicament we can find ourselves in as we ask different questions and begin to experience the change those questions can bring. Remember, when we are anxious our cerebral cortex is often short-circuited, so it cannot exercise the rational function it usually provides. We become reactive, making thoughtful discussion and action impossible. Sometimes the cortex is highjacked by the amygdala and used to support a fight response with a rationale for actions that are not reasoned or reasonable. When this happens there can be all sorts of fallout. Battles erupt. Accusations are made. Either/or thinking predominates. Blaming becomes rampant. The marginalization, diversion, attack, and seduction that Heifetz and Linsky describe become commonplace. It is likely that you as a leader will be the recipient of most of this. It happens. And it hurts. Your motives are questioned. Your values are attacked. Your skills are critiqued. Your faith is found wanting. You are not even the real issue, but you can say, "It's not about me" all you want, and it still hurts.

What others do to us is part of the predicament we may find ourselves in as we attempt to lead a congregation to the new questions. The other part is what we ourselves do or do not do. The challenges are great here, as well. In chapter 1, we looked at the importance of maintaining a nonanxious presence in an anxious system. That's not easy to do when you feel under attack, when your motives, values, skills, and faith are being questioned. Responding, not reacting, is essential, however. When you react, you contribute to the spiraling descent of the congregation into dysfunction. In his discussion of this phenomenon, Peter Steinke names several behaviors that will help us avoid this descent. We need to learn to:

- manage our own natural reactions;
- use knowledge to support impulses and control automatic reactions;
- keep calm for the purpose of reflection and conversation;
- observe what is happening, especially with oneself;
- tolerate high degrees of uncertainty, frustration, and pain;
- maintain a clear sense of direction.[4]

Our ability to do these things will enhance the possibility of helping the congregation deal with its anxiety and stress. Conversely, our inability to do them will contribute to the already anxious and stressful situation. Nobody utilizes these behaviors perfectly, but our inability to act consistently within these parameters can be a problem, not just for us but for the entire congregation.

Yet practicing these behaviors can lead to new challenges for us. If we maintain a clear sense of direction, refusing to get misdirected by the demands of others and the consistent messages about what we should be doing, we will likely be seen by some as a shirker, incompetent, and a failure as a pastor for not attending to the work they believe we should be about; some will see us as arrogant, opinionated, and determined to get our own way in all things. As leaders, we have to accept the fact that this is quite likely to happen. I became aware of this in my own ministry as I was attempting to lead a congregation to address some internal dynamics that threated the significant growth that had taken place. As the tensions increased, I came to the realization that in order to be the pastor they really needed at that time, I had to stay focused on the issues I was attempting to address and to do that for as long as I could in a way that didn't jeopardize my health or the well-being of my family or the congregation. If I could, then the congregation might be able to move beyond the dysfunction that plagued it, so that the next pastor would be in a better position to lead effectively and faithfully. The difficult reality I had to accept was that if I succeeded and things settled down after I left, many people would probably say, "See, the problem was Jeff all along." I'm not certain my ego ever let me fully accept that reality, but knowing it was needed allowed me to help some people in the congregation engage the important issues they needed to address.

Insight into another dimension of the predicament comes from Margaret Wheatley, an organizational consultant and author who draws on science as a way to understand leadership. In her book *So Far from Home*, she says she used to think she could change the world—that by doing what she did and helping others do it, she could make a profound difference in the direction the world was headed so that it would be more just and caring. She no longer believes that is possible, because "powerful, life-destroying dynamics have been set in motion that cannot be stopped. We're on a disastrous course with each other and with the planet. We've lost track of our best human qualities and forgotten the real sources of satisfaction, meaning and joy."[5] That, I admit, is a pretty dismal view of things. For Wheatley, it is based in her understanding of emergence theory. This theory maintains that change happens in a way that is actually beyond the control of humans as it begins to influence our behaviors.

> At the beginning, each part is acting in isolation, making decisions based on its own needs. But as separate elements start to connect with one another, emergence begins. Individual actions that were insignificant start to have new consequences because they are interconnected. At some point, a system will emerge with new and surprising properties that, from that point on, will profoundly influence the behaviors of the individual parts.[6]

But there's more: "Once something has emerged, it's here to stay. The only way to create something different is to start over, to begin again."[7] Thus, Wheatley believes, attempts to adjust the system are doomed to fail; the only option is the emergence of another system. Neither does it do any good to deny the existence of the system that has emerged. It is the reality with which we must deal.

My purpose in sharing this is not to depress you, but to call attention to the predicament in which her understanding of our current situation leaves both Wheatley and us. She writes: "It saddens me to see how many are still locked down by the belief that if they just work a little harder, if they just collaborate better or build a bigger network, if they just develop a new approach, they'll turn the world around. Can we please abandon these self-destructive beliefs?"[8] Without having to agree completely with Wheatley's assessment of the state of the world, we can still see the point of her concern. This is no longer a time in which doing the things we have done before will work. The former things, the old ways of dealing with things, are ineffective, if not counterproductive. This means that the old standards by which we gauge our effectiveness and success are no longer valid; they may now in fact be self-destructive. Faced with that reality, we, along with Wheatley, need to abandon our old ways and standards and find a deeper reason to be about the work we are doing, a new way to determine if the things we are about are really worth it. If it is no longer possible to save the world or transform the congregation or increase worship attendance or achieve greater financial viability, what brings meaning to what we do? If the old standards by which we (and most others) judge our success no longer mean anything, are there new ones and, if so, what are they?

In many ways, this book presents new ways of shaping our understanding of being about what matters most in these days. The need we face is to send people into the world to serve others using the gifts they have been given to work in ways we have discerned that make the reign of God more fully present amid the chaos and confusion, dislocation and destruction of the world. It's about doing whatever we can wherever we happen to be to share in God's work of redeeming all creation. It's not bringing in the reign of God completely or redeeming all creation, but simply doing our bit. That's what we are about as leaders in the church. That's what congregations themselves should be about.

But if we are honest, we also need to admit that there are any number of congregations that will not be able to make these changes. No leader, no plan, nothing will enable them to think and act that differently. You may well be the pastor or a member of such a congregation. You may even have a strong sense that there are real possibilities for the future of the congregation, if only they could bring themselves to do the necessary things. But they just can't do that. If this is where you find yourself, it's essential to avoid falling into frustration and reactivity. It's essential to remember that, as the fate of the Jerusalem temple reminds us, God is not about institutional survival. I am certain that God had a deeper and longer relationship with the Jerusalem temple than with any congregation or denomination around today. If the temple could fall, so can any religious institution. With this in mind, it becomes possible to accept the reality of the situation, to avoid falling into blaming others or yourself. It's not that the people of the congregation lack faith or vision or courage. It's not that you are not skilled enough, knowledgeable enough, or motivated enough to lead them. It is simply that institutional survival is not what matters most. All institutions are temporary. God is about something much more significant.

Now the challenge that comes to us in moving beyond a traditional view of congregations and why it creates a predicament for us is that it is exceedingly difficult to let go of those old standards that were once the markers for ministry. We need to let go of increased worship attendance, let go of bigger budgets, let go of the dream of being recognized by the denomination as a turnaround pastor, let go of the desire to move on to a bigger church, let go of restructuring according to the latest standards of organizational efficiency and effectiveness, let go of pithy and memorable mission statements, let go of maintaining the historically significant church building. All of that and much more we may well need to let go because they are no longer indicators of the kind of success that really matters. In fact, we need to let go of results all together. What we need to reclaim, hold on to, and never let go is doing the right thing, because it is the thing that God has called us to do, the good deed God has already prepared for us to do, the way we play our part in the redemption of all creation. Thomas Merton said:

> Do not depend on the hope of results. When you are doing the sort of work you have taken on, essentially an apostolic work, you may have to face the fact that your work will be apparently worthless and even achieve no result at all, if not perhaps results opposite to what you expect. As you get used to this idea, you start more and more to concentrate not on the results, but on the value, the rightness, the truth of the work itself.[9]

That's it!

Don't underestimate the extent of the challenge required to come to terms with letting go of the old standards. It's a great challenge because our own egos are in many ways linked to those old standards. It's also a great challenge because those standards shape the expectations people, who if we are clergy pay us and contribute to our pension funds, have for what pastors should do. This is what Robert Quinn, whose work we looked at in chapter 3, calls deep change. Leading deep change in a congregation is hard work. It is also hard to reach a point where you understand deep change is not possible and, as Quinn points out, the only alternative is slow death. Slow death comes when we ignore the realities and limit the possibilities, when we are passive in the face of the challenges we face, when we have no hope that God is up to something bigger. There are some congregations for whom slow death is the only possibility. But even in that God is present and at work. Whatever our setting, Quinn speaks clearly about what it takes to lead effectively. "The problem is that to grow, to take the journeys on which our growth is predicated, we must confront our own immaturity, selfishness, and lack of courage."[10]

Are you ready for that?

Finally, we need to recognize that the predicament we find ourselves in is ultimately the fault of the Holy Spirit. As we seek to discern what God is up to, the way in which we can be involved in the redemption of all creation, all those things we have talked about in this book, it is the Holy Spirit that is our only true guide. The Holy Spirit is the one who makes the every-five-hundred-year rummage sale a necessity, because the Holy Spirit is relentlessly moving us and the church into the world as it really is, so that we can bring the love of God to that world in a way that heals the hurt, soothes the suffering, addresses the addiction, and intercedes in the injustice. As good as doing all this work sounds, there is a problem. You see, the Holy Spirit never does anything decently and in good order. If we are attentive to the Holy Spirit, we need to be comfortable with chaos and willing to embrace disorder—and not just us, the church itself. As theologian Daniel Migliore has noted, "The institutional church has always looked on the experience of and appeal to the Spirit as potentially subversive and in need of control."[11] In the church today there is a compelling need to be at least a little bit subversive, a desperate need to give up control. There is, in other words, a need for the Holy Spirit.

This is our predicament.

# 10

# THE PRAYER

In light of everything I dealt with in the last chapter, you may be tempted to simply surrender to the old adage, "You haven't got a prayer." Thankfully, however, prayer is one of the things we always have. Prayer is very much in order, for the key to seeing our way through the predicaments described in chapter 9 (and the myriad other predicaments that will inevitably arise) is to foster deep spiritual lives.

We can draw on other resources that may help to some extent, but in the final analysis our ability to lead effectively in the midst of the predicaments we face comes down to the depth of our spiritual lives. It does help immeasurably to be attentive to self-care. It makes a big difference when we have interests and friends unrelated to our church responsibilities. Dealing with our own family of origin, as family systems theory suggests, will help us avoid bringing our own issues into a situation. Insight for dealing with these predicaments can come from the Myers-Briggs Type Indicator and the Enneagram.

Ronald Heifetz and Marty Linsky offer some additional insight. They remind us of the personal dimension of leadership, advising us to "manage our hungers" by attending to our need for power and control, affirmation and importance, and intimacy and delight in settings unrelated to our leadership position, so that these concerns will not become issues in our ministry.[1] In their view, "anchoring" ourselves is also vital to effective leadership—something we accomplish by learning to distinguish the role we play from the persons we are, nurturing relationships with confidants who are not related to our ministry, and seeking a place of sanctuary where through reflection and renewal we can reaffirm a deeper sense of self and purpose.[2]

Margaret Wheatley points out the importance of kindred spirits, reminding us, "We need each other, our small circle of other valiant ones. We can too easily lose our way if we don't stop for occasional conversations where we remember what first called to us, what we still love, where we find satisfaction however small and momentary. We need time together to comfort, support and console one another."[3]

These insights and those of many other leadership theorists can be a tremendous help in dealing with the predicaments we face, but they are not enough. Even secular writers acknowledge this and speak of the need for a spiritual dimension to leadership.

In writing about the essential need for deep change in organizations and those who lead them, Robert Quinn states: "Ultimately, deep change, whether at the personal or the organizational level, is a spiritual process."[4] The work we are about needs to be aligned with our values and true purpose in order to be meaningful. This alignment can be lost over time as we gradually focus on the wrong things in order to achieve the results we seek. So, for example, assuming that we cannot really be a church without a building, we may direct our resources to the maintenance of the building, rather than a mission that shares God's love in the world, and become more and more inwardly focused. As this happens, we develop rationales for the actions we have taken and the results that have occurred. Quinn asserts that the journey back from the slow death to which this lack of alignment leads is a difficult one:

> To thwart our defense mechanisms and bypass slow death, we must confront first our own hypocrisy and cowardice. We must recognize the lies we have been telling ourselves. We must acknowledge our own weakness, greed, insensitivity, and lack of vision and courage. If we do so, we begin to understand the clear need for a course correction, and we slowly begin to reinvent our self. The transition is painful, and we are often hesitant, fearing we lack the courage and confidence

to proceed. . . . [But] the journey puts us on a path of exhilaration, growth and progress.[5]

Although expressed in secular terms, this is certainly a description of a spiritual journey.

Heifetz and Linsky are explicit in their use of a religious image as they describe the way of a leader. They begin by asking why we do it—why we engage in leadership when it can be so difficult, even painful, at times. Their answer is that we do it for love and the deeper meaning love brings to our lives and the lives of others. The image of love that they share is the sacred heart.

Ron, who is Jewish, tells the story of his discovery of the meaning of the sacred heart. It happened in an Anglican church in England on the eve of Rosh Hashanah. He concludes his story with these words:

> That's what we learned about sacred heart—the willingness to feel everything, everything, to hold it all without letting go of your work. To feel, as Reb Jesus felt, the gravest doubt, forsaken and betrayed near his moment of death. To cry out like King David in the wilderness, just when you desperately want to believe that you're doing the right thing, that your sacrifice means something, "My God, my God, why have you forsaken me?" But in nearly the same instant, to feel compassion, "Father, forgive them for they know not what they do."

Then he describes what the sacred heart means for life and leadership:

> A sacred heart means you may feel tortured and betrayed, powerless and hopeless, and yet stay open. It's the capacity to encompass the entire range of your human experience without hardening or closing yourself. It means that even in the midst of disappointment and defeat, you remain connected to people and to the sources of your most profound purposes.[6]

So, how does this happen? How do we come to the point where we are the people who can act in the way that Heifetz describes? Becoming this kind of person is, I believe, the essence of all spiritual growth. The spiritual journey enables us to become the person who lives in this way.

Spiritual growth is, of course, a long and continuing process. It involves struggle and uncertainty, a good bit of falling short and backsliding, and it is never completed. But this journey of the spirit makes life worth living and faithful leadership possible. There are no easy fixes, no shortcuts. There is a good measure of pain and suffering involved. It takes time, decades really. To provide the leadership that is needed in congregations, to do what we have talked about in this book, we need to undertake this spiritual journey. Without doing so, we will be too self-absorbed, too dependent on the opinions of others, too tied up in our own ego needs to lead as we need to lead.

Brian McLaren puts the need for the journey this way: "'You can't give what you don't have,' which means, before anything else, we who lead must actually embody the Spirit-saturated, Christ-following, God-loving way of life we hope to pass on through our churches. To become like Christ we need to have the Spirit of Christ within us, among us, before us, beside us, as the old Celtic prayer says. We need to be Spirit-saturated people."[7]

It is, of course, impossible to describe precisely and fully the impact taking this spiritual journey will have for us. Each journey is unique and expansive. No list of lessons from the journey could ever be complete. For our purposes, however, I would like to consider five lessons that have been particularly significant for me and others with whom I have talked. The lessons, or perhaps more accurately gifts, of the spiritual journey that have led to significant change in my living and leading are patience, discovering the importance of struggle, fortitude, new purpose, and peace.

*Patience.* I learned patience through the spiritual journey because I needed to be patient with myself. I had to be patient or I would have given up for lack of results. I found it hard to follow through on the disciplines I adopted. I had to sort through the disciplines that were available to discover ones that resonated best with me and my nature. I had to learn that just because a discipline didn't come easily didn't mean that it couldn't be helpful. I had to realize that the process was slow, that it involves both steps forward and steps back, and that it in fact never really ends. I had to accept the reality that for much of the journey, it seemed I wasn't traveling very well at all. I had to learn to relish the times when everything fell together and let those experiences sustain me when everything fell apart. I had to struggle with my need to control and decide, my reluctance to let go. I had to be patient with myself, hoping that my belief that God was infinitely patient with me was true.

One perspective that helped me learn patience came from the writing of Richard Rohr. In a recent book, *Falling Upward*, he focuses explicitly on a theme that runs throughout his writing: many of the changes we seek in our spiritual growth are attainable only in the second half of life. In the first half of life we need to be attentive to ourselves, our own identity, purpose, and relationships, which, he says, provide the "container" for our lives. In the second half of life, our challenge is to fill that container with our true and unique selves. The first half of life task is shaped by others and the world we live in and leads to the development of what Rohr terms "the False Self," because it is shaped by those external forces. In the second half of life, we turn to the development of "the True Self," which is the unique person that God created us to be. As we become more this True Self, we are able to let go of the need to please the external forces and to prove ourselves. If we are not able to leave the False Self of our early years behind, we are continually beholden to the opinions of others, we continually strive to prove that we are capable, we are unable to shape our own purpose and direction because we are still living according to what others (be they parents, mentors, or parishioners) want us to be and do. If we continue to live as a False Self, our ability to lead a congregation, to ask new questions, and to act in different ways is seriously compromised. Rohr provides the perspective of time, which has helped me to understand the long-term nature of the spiritual journey and to recognize that I simply have to wait for some aspects of the journey to become possible for me. That doesn't mean we just wait until a mid-life crisis propels us into the second half of life, however, for much growth can happen in our early years, but it does help us recognize that the journey is a lifelong one for which patience is required.

The wondrous benefit of developing patience with ourselves is that we become more patient with others. Knowing something about how difficult growth and change is for us helps us understand the reasons others struggle and often resist. We are more able to accept them as they are, while at the same time encouraging their change and growth. This patience is an important attribute as we work with people in a congregation. The aspects of faith they hold dear are difficult to let go, so patience is needed. Institutions are even more difficult to change, so even more patience is needed. We can be patient, because in our spiritual journey we have encountered a God who accepts us just as we are while always calling us to be something more.

*Discovering the Importance of Struggle.* I don't like to suffer. I would prefer not to have to struggle with anything. Unfortunately, life inevitably involves both suffering and struggle. There was a time when I believed the best way to deal with suffering and struggle was to tough it out, to put on my stoic New England persona and grin and bear it. That ended when the struggle became unbearable. The first major struggle in my life came during my senior year in college. I was, in Rohr's terms, very much in a container-building mode, but even so, I knew that the container I was building would not do the job of providing a foundation for my living. So I redirected my life, attempting to build it on a more solid foundation. Through this experience I began to see not just that suffering was unavoidable, but that it held within it the possibility of change and growth. Rohr provides insight:

> Sooner or later, if you are on any classic "spiritual schedule," some event, person, death, idea, or relationship will enter your life that you simply cannot deal with, using your present skill set, your acquired knowledge, or your strong willpower. Spiritually speaking, you will be, you must be, led to the edge of your own private resources. At that point you will stumble over a necessary stumbling stone, as Isaiah calls it. . . . This is the only way that Life-Fate-God-Grace-Mystery can get you to change, let go of your egocentric preoccupations, and go on the further and larger journey. I wish I could say this was not true, but it is darn near absolute in the spiritual literature of the world. [8]

It is only when we experience and acknowledge the pain and suffering we encounter that we are able to engage the deep issues of life and faith in order to discover the truth they hold. But, as Rohr notes, "Before the truth 'sets you free,' it tends to make you miserable."[9]

So, perhaps, the spiritual journey begins (or can only truly begin) as our world starts to fall apart and we experience the pain, struggle, and suffering that come with that. As we encounter our fraying world, both because of what we have done and what has happened to us, true spiritual growth becomes possible.

It can be that a ministry in a congregation in which we seek to ask new questions will create a struggle, perhaps even lead to suffering. We can never be certain what the level of resistance to change will be. If struggle does occur, if we suffer because of it, then, even in the midst of the pain we may experience, the spiritual journey we are on will help us look for ways the struggle and suffering will enhance that journey and make us more able to endure.

In this we begin to see the true, illogical, utterly wondrous work of the Spirit. For the predicaments that require our spiritual growth if we are to survive them, are, at the very same time, the gateways into that growth. It's not automatic and it doesn't happen easily but the opportunity is there for us if we take it, if we have the faith and hope to do so. The struggle, the suffering, the pain we may endure is redeemed and in that we experience the power of God that is for us most certainly, but also at work in all creation. If we can experience that in a congregation then it truly becomes a crucible of hope.

*Fortitude.* The college struggle that sent me in a new direction wasn't the only time in my life I experienced suffering. Personally and professionally there have been times of uncertainty and doubt, times of rejection and pain, times when death intruded and I wondered what life would now be like. As the spiritual journey continued I endured and in that endurance found a fortitude that kept me going. I discovered in the midst of one of the significant struggles of my ministry that I could endure in the simple faith that God was up to something. I didn't know what God was up to and I didn't know when I would learn, but I trusted, which meant I had hope even in the midst of difficult times. I just kept saying to myself and anyone who asked how I was doing, "God is up to something."

Joan Chittister, a Roman Catholic nun, writes about the importance of struggle in our personal growth in her book *Scarred by Struggle, Transformed by Hope*. These are, she says, the times when the ways in which we have shaped our lives no longer work and we are left searching for something more. Through this struggle, she maintains, we become fully ourselves, more fully the persons God created us to be. The inner strength we gradually acquire, the reduced dependency on results and lack of dependence on the views of others means that we can persevere in situations that do not seem to lend themselves to traditional standards of success. Chittister writes, "[Endurance] is the willingness to keep on doing what must be done because doing it is meaningful, is worthy of us, and more than equals the struggle it takes to do it."[10] We can endure because we have gained an insight into what really matters in the ongoing spiritual journey: "It is not a matter of changing what cannot be changed. It is a matter of refusing to allow what ought to be changed to conform us to itself."[11] It is enough, in the framework of this book, to keep asking the questions that matter.

*New Purpose.* My college struggle led to a new purpose for my life and started me on a new spiritual journey. That isn't the only time this has happened, however. Throughout the journey I have discovered that my growth deepened upon letting go of old ways of thinking about what I was to do so that I could open myself to the new ways God had in store for me. I have had to let go of purposes related to my own advancement and the image I had of myself as a successful pastor. Sometimes I let go of them because I discovered they simply didn't work. Sometimes I didn't let go: sometimes whatever I was clinging to was taken from me. Each time, however, a new purpose emerged that gave me a different and deeper way to direct my ministry.

I have shared my belief that to lead effectively in today's church, we need to let go of the old standards we used to assess our ministry and our success as pastors. Increased attendance and increased giving can no longer serve that purpose. Preaching to adoring multitudes probably won't make it for most of us either. They are among the criteria of success that we need to let go and put in the rummage sale.

We need to set those criteria aside so we can accept the hard reality that some, perhaps many, congregations will die in the coming years because they have not been able to make the changes that are essential for survival. We may well be the leaders in those congregations. If we can see this death not so much as someone's fault or a failing on our part, but rather as the natural evolution of God's unfolding purpose, we are able to accept the death of specific congregations, as difficult and painful as that can be for us, as part of a process in which God's work is done, God's love is shared more fully in the world. But note well: we are able to hold this perspective only if we have already set aside the usual standards of success and embraced the reality that the reign of God is not really about institution building, maintenance, or survival. It is only possible if we have already undertaken the journey of the spirit that leads us to a new purpose.

*Peace.* Peace is hard to come by. The world is in turmoil. Congregations struggle to survive. Personal relationships endure conflict and tension. Simply reading the newspaper creates a dis-ease of the spirit. And yet, peace is one of the gifts of the spiritual journey. Perhaps we know peace only partially. Perhaps it exists alongside an uneasiness that ebbs and flows. As we continue on the journey our experience of peace may become more frequent, but few of us will fully know the peace we seek. There are still days my stomach is in turmoil; still nights I cannot sleep. But there is also a sense of peace even then. For me peace is not an all-or-nothing experience, and it probably never will be. But the journey I have been on makes it possible to let go of the angst more often and more fully than I previously could. I am more able to let go and trust that if the whole world is in God's hands, I'm probably there too.

This peace, even if we experience it fleetingly, strengthens our spirits and our leadership in the congregation. I don't know exactly why I am able to experience peace in times of congregational struggle or when my frustration is high and nothing I do seems to work. I guess that is one of the reasons it is the peace that passes understanding. I do know that this

peace is present and real, however. And I do know that it makes a difference in who I am and what I do.

The more we enter into this peace that we cannot understand, the more
we are able to embrace the fullness of our experience, both good and bad,
and let go of those struggles and concerns that bring distress. In the
experience of the peace of God, we learn, in the words of Richard Rohr,
"how to hold creative tensions, how to live with paradox and contradic-
tions, how not to run from mystery, and therefore how to practice what all
religions teach as necessary: compassion, mercy, loving kindness, patience, forgiveness, and humility."[12]

When that happens we not only experience peace, we become peace-
makers.

God is love. I suppose that means that the ultimate goal of our spiritual
journey is love. We experience love along the way, of course, but the
further along we go, the more open we are both to receive and share love.
Dallas Willard writes about the importance of continuing to grow in this
love:

> Taking love itself—God's kind of love—into the depths of our being
> through spiritual formation will . . . enable us to act lovingly to an
> extent that will be surprising even to ourselves, at first. And this love
> will then become a constant source of joy and refreshment to ourselves
> and others.[13]

It is in that faith that we minister, relying on God's love to sustain us
and knowing that no matter the difficulties we face, there is always a
prayer:

> I pray that, according to the riches of his glory, he may grant that you
> may be strengthened in your inner being with power through his Spirit,
> and that Christ may dwell in your hearts through faith, as you are being
> rooted and grounded in love. I pray that you may have the power to
> comprehend, with all the saints, what is the breadth and length and
> height and depth, and to know the love of Christ that surpasses knowl-

edge, so that you may be filled with all the fullness of God. (Ephesians 3:16–19)

May you know this love in all that you do, believing that it is God's love and it is for you. May the congregations of which you are a part know this love as well. May they share this love with each other and a world in desperate need, that they may truly be crucibles of hope.

# NOTES

## INTRODUCTION

1. Margaret Wheatley, *So Far From Home: Lost and Found in Our Brave New World* (San Francisco: Berrett Koehler, 2012), 150.

## 1. THE PROBLEM WITH POOL TABLES AND WHAT THAT MEANS FOR US

1. Thomas G. Bandy, *Kicking Habits: Welcome Relief for Addicted Churches*, upgrade ed. (Nashville: Abingdon, 2001).

2. Clifford Geertz, *The Interpretation of Cultures: Selected Essays by Clifford Geertz* (New York: Basic Books, 1973), 89.

3. Geertz, *The Interpretation of Cultures*, 99.

4. Peter L. Steinke, *Congregational Leadership in Anxious Times: Being Calm and Courageous No Matter What* (Herndon, VA: Alban, 2006), 12.

5. Robert Kegan and Lisa Laskow Lahey, *How the Way We Talk Can Change the Way We Work* (San Francisco: Jossey-Bass, 2002); Robert Kegan and Lisa Laskow Lahey, *Immunity to Change* (San Francisco: Jossey-Bass, 2009).

6. William Willimon, *Acts* (Atlanta: John Knox Press, 1988), 55.

7. Steinke, *Congregational Leadership in Anxious Times*, 31.

8. Ronald A. Heifetz and Marty Linsky, *Leadership on the Line: Staying Alive through the Dangers of Leading* (Boston: Harvard Business School Press, 2002), 102–3.

9. Heifetz and Linsky, *Leadership on the Line*, 102.


# 2. WHY EZRA AND NEHEMIAH WERE WRONG AND WHAT THAT MEANS FOR US

1. This insight and much of the following discussion are based on the work of Paul D. Hanson in *The Dawn of Apocalyptic: The Historical and Sociological Roots of Jewish Apocalyptic Eschatology, revised edition* (Philadelphia: Fortress, 1979).

2. Paul D. Hanson, "Israelite Religion in the Early Postexilic Period," in *Ancient Israelite Religion: Essays in Honor of Frank Moore Cross*, ed. Patrick D. Miller et al. (Philadelphia: Fortress, 1987), 493–94.

3. Hanson, *The Dawn of Apocalyptic*, 72–73.

4. Hanson, *The Dawn of Apocalyptic*, 247.

5. Hanson, *The Dawn of Apocalyptic*, 170.


# 3. BUT WAIT! THERE'S MORE!

1. Robert E. Quinn, *Deep Change: Discovering the Leader Within* (San Francisco: Jossey-Bass, 1996), 3.

2. Phyllis Tickle, *The Great Emergence: How Christianity Is Changing and Why* (Grand Rapids: Baker, 2008).

3. Phyllis Tickle, *Emergence Christianity: What It Is, Where It Is Going, and Why It Matters* (Grand Rapids: Baker, 2012), 25.

4. Tickle, *The Great Emergence*, 17.

5. Diana Butler Bass, *Christianity after Religion: The End of Church and the Birth of a New Spiritual Awakening* (New York: HarperOne, 2012).

6. Gerhard Von Rad, *The Message of the Prophets*, trans. D. M. G. Stalker (New York: Harper and Row, 1967), 9.

7. Von Rad, *The Message of the Prophets*, 9.

8. Von Rad, *The Message of the Prophets*, 10.

9. Von Rad, *The Message of the Prophets*, 10.

## PART 2 INTRODUCTION

1. Max Depree, *Leadership Is an Art* (New York: Doubleday, 1989), 9.

2. Robert Kegan and Lisa Laskow Lahey, *How the Way We Talk Can Change the Way We Work* (San Francisco: Jossey-Bass, 2002); Robert Kegan and Lisa Laskow Lahey, *Immunity to Change* (San Francisco: Jossey-Bass, 2009).

3. Edwin Friedman, *A Failure of Nerve: Leadership in the Age of the Quick Fix* (New York: Seabury, 2007), 37.

4. Rainer Maria Rilke, *Letters to a Young Poet*, trans. Reginald Snell (Mineola, NY: Dover Publications, 2002), 21.

## 4. IN/OUT

1. Unitarian Universalist Associate, www.uua.org/growth/breakthrough/144088.shtml.

2. Thomas G. Bandy, *Kicking Habits: Welcome Relief for Addicted Churches*, upgrade edition (Nashville: Abingdon, 2001), 43–113.

3. Darrell L. Gruder, "From Sending to Being Sent," in *Missional Church: A Vision for the Sending of the Church in North America,* edited by Darrell L. Gruder, 1–17 (Grand Rapids: Eerdmans, 1998), 77.

4. See George Hunsburger, "Missional Vocation: Called and Sent to Represent the Reign of God," in *Missional Church: A Vision for the Sending of the Church in North America*, edited by Darrell L. Gruder, 77–109 (Grand Rapids: Eerdmans, 1998).

5. Gruder, *Missional Church*, 4–5.

6. Personal translation inspired in large measure by one offered by Dallas Willard. See Dallas Willard, *The Great Omission: Reclaiming Jesus's Essential Teachings on Discipleship* (New York: HarperCollins, 2006), xiii.

7. Willard, *The Great Omission*, xix.

8. Willard, *The Great Omission*, xv.

9. A full description of these elements of discipleship can be found in Jeffrey D. Jones, *Traveling Together: A Guide for Disciple-Forming Congregations* (Herndon, VA: Alban, 2006).

## 5. PASTOR/CONGREGATION

1. Alan J. Roxburgh, "Missional Leadership: Equipping God's People for Mission," in *Missional Church: A Vision for the Sending of the Church in North America*, ed. Darrell L. Gruder (Grand Rapids: Eerdmans, 1998), 191.

2. Roxburgh, "Missional Leadership," 195.

3. See Roxburgh, "Missional Leadership," 190–95, for a more detailed discussion of the impact of traditional clergy roles on laity and the life of the congregation.

4. Tony Jones, *The Church Is Flat: The Relational Ecclesiology of the Emerging Church Movement* (Minneapolis: The JoPa Group, 2011), Kindle edition, location 166.

5. Tony Jones in *The Church Is Flat* offers a discussion of Moltmann's ecclesiology that introduces the themes that are central to this discussion. As is often the case, Tony's thinking stimulated my own in some important ways.

6. Jürgen Moltmann, *Sun of Righteousness Arise!: God's Future for Humanity and the Earth* (Minneapolis: Fortress, 2010), 21.

7. Moltmann, *Sun of Righteousness*, 22–23.

8. Moltmann, *Sun of Righteousness*, 24.

9. Moltmann, *Sun of Righteousness*, 24–25.

10. C. Jeff Woods, *Congregational Megatrends* (Herndon, VA: Alban, 1996).

11. Woods, 137.

## 6. PLANNED/DISCERNED

1. Danny Morris and Charles M. Olsen, *Discerning God's Will Together: A Spiritual Practice for the Church* (Nashville: Upper Room Books, 1997), 23.

2. Suzanne G. Farnham, Stephanie A. Hull, and R. Taylor McLean. *Grounded in God: Listening Hearts Discernment for Group Deliberations* (Harrisburg: Morehouse, 1999), 6.

3. Pierre Wolff, *Discernment: The Art of Choosing Well*, revised edition (Liguori, MO: Liguori/Triumph, 2003), 7.

4. The items listed here provide one way of looking at the discernment process. Additional helpful resources that more fully explore corporate discernment include *Grounded in God* by Suzanne G. Farnham, Stephanie A. Hull, and R. Taylor McLean, and *Discerning God's Will Together* by Danny L. Morris and Charles M. Olsen. There is also a helpful chapter on group discernment in *Discernment: The Art of Choosing Well* by Pierre Wolff.

5. Morris and Olsen, *Discerning God's Will Together*, 44.

6. Peter Senge, *The Fifth Discipline: The Art and Practice of The Learning Organization* (New York: Doubleday, 1990), 238–49, referenced in Morris and Olsen, *Discerning God's Will Together*, 70.

7. Farnham et al., *Grounded in God*, 6.

8. Farnham et al., *Grounded in God*, 28.


## 7. SURVIVE/SERVE

1. Pierre Wolff, *Discernment: The Art of Choosing Well*, revised ed. (Liguori, MO: Liguori/Triumph, 2003), 21.

2. Peter L. Steinke, *Congregational Leadership in Anxious Times: Being Calm and Courageous No Matter What* (Herndon, VA: Alban, 2006), 121.

3. David Ray, *The Indispensable Guide for Smaller Churches* (Cleveland: Pilgrim Press, 2003), 60.

4. Jürgen Moltmann, *The Church and the Power of the Holy Spirit: A Contribution to Messianic Ecclesiology*, trans. Margaret Kohl (London: SCM Press, 1977), 19.


## 8. SAVE/SIGN

1. N. T. Wright, *Jesus and the Victory of God: Christian Origins and the Question of God*, vol. 2 (Philadelphia: Fortress, 1996), 469.

2. Kevin G. Ford, *Transforming Church: Bringing Out the Good to Get to Great* (Carol Stream, IL: Tyndale, 2007), 57.

3. Ford, *Transforming Church*, 83.

4. Ford, *Transforming Church*, 83.

5. Ford, *Transforming Church*, 84.

6. Ford, *Transforming Church*, 84.

7. Ford, *Transforming Church*, 74.

## 9. THE PREDICAMENT

1. Ronald A. Heifetz and Marty Linsky, *Leadership on the Line: Staying Alive through the Dangers of Leading* (Boston: Harvard Business School Press, 2002).

2. Heifetz and Linsky, *Leadership on the Line*, 31–48.

3. Heifetz and Linsky, *Leadership on the Line*, 48.

4. Peter L. Steinke, *Congregational Leadership in Anxious Times: Being Calm and Courageous No Matter What* (Herndon, VA: Alban, 2006), 35.

5. Margaret Wheatley, *So Far From Home: Lost and Found in Our Brave New World* (San Francisco: Berrett-Koehler, 2012), 5.

6. Wheatley, *So Far From Home*, 30.

7. Wheatley, *So Far From Home*, 32.

8. Wheatley, *So Far From Home*, 35.

9. Thomas Merton, "A letter written to James Forest, February 21, 1966," in *The Hidden Ground of Love: The Letters of Thomas Merton on Religious Experience and Social Concerns*, ed. William Shannon (New York: Farrar, Strauss and Giroux, 1993), 294.

10. Robert E. Quinn, *Deep Change: Discovering the Leader Within* (San Francisco: Jossey-Bass, 1996), 37.

11. Daniel L. Migliore, *Faith Seeking Understanding: An Introduction to Christian Theology*, second edition (Grand Rapids: Eerdmans, 2004), 224.

## 10. THE PRAYER

1. Ronald A. Heifetz and Marty Linsky, *Leadership on the Line: Staying Alive through the Dangers of Leading* (Boston: Harvard Business School Press, 2002), 163–86.

2. Heifetz and Linsky, *Leadership on the Line*, 187–206.

3. Margaret Wheatley, *So Far From Home: Lost and Found in Our Brave New World* (San Francisco: Berrett-Koehler, 2012), 150.

4. Robert E. Quinn, *Deep Change: Discovering the Leader Within* (San Francisco: Jossey-Bass, 1996), 78.

5. Quinn, *Deep Change*, 78.

6. Heifetz and Linsky, *Leadership on the Line,* 229–30.

7. Brian D. McLaren, *A New Kind of Christianity: Ten Questions That Are Transforming the Faith* (New York: HarperCollins, 2010), 165.

8. Richard Rohr, *Falling Upward: A Spirituality for the Two Halves of Life* (San Francisco: Jossey-Bass, 2011), Kindle edition, 65, location 1240.

9. Rohr, *Falling Upward*, 74/location 1341.

10. Joan Chittister, *Scarred by Struggle, Transformed by Hope* (Grand Rapids: Eerdmans, 2003), Kindle edition, location 1027.

11. Chittister, *Scarred by Struggle*, location 1301.

12. Richard Rohr, *The Naked Now: Learning to See as the Mystics See* (New York: Crossroad, 2009), 132.

13. Dallas Willard, *Renovation of the Heart: Putting on the Character of Christ* (Colorado Springs: NavPress, 2002), 24.

# BIBLIOGRAPHY

Bandy, Thomas G. *Kicking Habits: Welcome Relief for Addicted Churches*, upgrade edition. Nashville: Abingdon, 2001.

Barrett, Lois. "Missional Witness: The Church as Apostle to the World." In *Missional Church: A Vision for the Sending of the Church in North America*, edited by Darrell L. Gruder, 110–41. Grand Rapids: Eerdmans, 1998.

Bass, Diana Butler. *Christianity after Religion: The End of Church and the Birth of a New Spiritual Awakening*. New York: HarperOne, 2012.

Chittister, Joan. *Scarred by Struggle, Transformed by Hope*. Grand Rapids: Eerdmans, 2003. Kindle edition.

Depree, Max. *Leadership Is an Art*. New York: Doubleday, 1989.

Farnham, Suzanne G., Stephanie A. Hull, and R. Taylor McLean. *Grounded in God: Listening Hearts Discernment for Group Deliberations*. Harrisburg: Morehouse, 1999.

Ford, Kevin G. *Transforming Church: Bringing Out the Good to Get to Great*. Carol Stream, IL: Tyndale, 2007.

Friedman, Edwin. *A Failure of Nerve: Leadership in the Age of the Quick Fix*. New York: Seabury, 2007.

Geertz, Clifford. *The Interpretation of Cultures: Selected Essays by Clifford Geertz*. New York: Basic Books, 1973.

Gruder, Darrell L., "From Sending to Being Sent." In *Missional Church: A Vision for the Sending of the Church in North America*, edited by Darrell L. Gruder, 1–17. Grand Rapids: Eerdmans, 1998.

Hanson, Paul D. *The Dawn of Apocalyptic: The Historical and Sociological Roots of Jewish Apocalyptic Eschatology, revised edition*. Philadelphia: Fortress, 1979.

———. "Israelite Religion in the Early Postexilic Period." In *Ancient Israelite Religion: Essays in Honor of Frank Moore Cross*, edited by Patrick D. Miller Jr., Paul D. Hanson, and S. Dean McBride, 485–508. Philadelphia: Fortress, 1987.

Heifetz, Ronald A., and Marty Linsky. *Leadership on the Line: Staying Alive through the Dangers of Leading*. Boston: Harvard Business School Press, 2002.

Hunsberger, George. "Missional Vocation: Called and Sent to Represent the Reign of God." In *Missional Church: A Vision for the Sending of the Church in North America*, edited by Darrell L. Gruder, 77–109. Grand Rapids: Eerdmans, 1998.

Jones, Jeffrey D. *Traveling Together: A Guide for Disciple-Forming Congregations.* Herndon, VA: Alban, 2006.

Jones, Tony. *The Church Is Flat: The Relational Ecclesiology of the Emerging Church Movement.* Minneapolis: The JoPa Group, 2011. Kindle edition.

Kegan, Robert, and Lisa Laskow Lahey. *How the Way We Talk Can Change the Way We Work.* San Francisco: Jossey-Bass, 2002.

———. *Immunity to Change.* San Francisco: Jossey-Bass, 2009.

McLaren, Brian D. *A New Kind of Christianity: Ten Questions that Are Transforming the Faith.* New York: HarperCollins, 2010.

Merton, Thomas. *The Hidden Ground of Love: The Letters of Thomas Merton on Religious Experience and Social Concerns.* Edited by William H. Shannon. New York: Farrar, Straus and Giroux, 1985.

Migliore, Daniel L. *Faith Seeking Understanding: An Introduction to Christian Theology*, 2nd edition. Grand Rapids: Eerdmans, 2004.

Moltmann, Jürgen. *The Church and the Power of the Holy Spirit: A Contribution to Messianic Ecclesiology.* Translated by Margaret Kohl. London: SCM Press, 1977.

———. *Sun of Righteousness Arise!: God's Future for Humanity and the Earth.* Translated by Margaret Kohl. Minneapolis: Fortress, 2010.

Morris, Danny, and Charles J. Olsen. *Discerning God's Will Together: A Spiritual Practice for the Church.* Nashville: Upper Room Books, 1997.

Quinn, Robert E. *Deep Change: Discovering the Leader Within.* San Francisco: Jossey-Bass, 1996.

Ray, David. *The Indispensable Guide for Smaller Churches.* Cleveland: Pilgrim Press, 2003.

Rilke, Rainer Maria. *Letters to a Young Poet.* Translated by Reginald Snell. Mineola, NY: Dover Publications, 2002.

Rohr, Richard. *The Naked Now: Learning to See as the Mystics See.* New York: Crossroad, 2009.

———. *Falling Upward: A Spirituality for the Two Halves of Life.* San Francisco: Jossey-Bass, 2011. Kindle edition.

Steinke, Peter L. *Congregational Leadership in Anxious Times: Being Calm and Courageous No Matter What.* Herndon, VA: Alban, 2006.

Tickle, Phyllis. *The Great Emergence: How Christianity Is Changing and Why.* Grand Rapids: Baker, 2008.

———. *Emergence Christianity: What It Is, Where It Is Going, and Why It Matters.* Grand Rapids: Baker, 2012.

Von Rad, Gerhard. *The Message of the Prophets.* Translated by D. M. G. Stalker. New York: Harper and Row, 1967.

Wheatley, Margaret. *So Far From Home: Lost and Found in Our Brave New World.* San Francisco: Berrett-Koehler, 2012.

Willard, Dallas. *Renovation of the Heart: Putting on the Character of Christ.* Colorado Springs: NavPress, 2002.

———. *The Great Omission: Reclaiming Jesus's Essential Teachings on Discipleship.* New York: HarperCollins, 2006.

Willimon, William. *Acts.* Atlanta: John Knox Press, 1988.

Wolff, Pierre. *Discernment: The Art of Choosing Well*, revised edition. Liguori, MO: Litguori/Triumph, 2003.

Woods, C. Jeff. *Congregational Megatrends.* Herndon, VA: Alban, 1996.

Wright, N. T. *Jesus and the Victory of God: Christian Origins and the Question of God*, Volume 2. Philadelphia: Fortress, 1996.